Practical Tips for

Woodturners

the best from WOODTURNING magazine

GMC Publications

First Published in 1994 by
Guild of Master Craftsman Publications Ltd,
Castle Place, 166 High Street, Lewes, East Sussex BN7 1XU

© GMC Publications Ltd 1994

ISBN 0 94619 74 2

Designed by GMC Design

Printed and bound in Great Britain by
Nuffield Press, Oxford.

CONTENTS

B

Bandsaw sharpener	7
Bobbin chuck (1)	7
Bobbin chuck (2)	7
Bowl design without waste	8
Bullnose centre	8
Bumper-outer	9

C

Centralising gadget	9
Centralising tool	10
Centre drills	10
Centre of gravity	11
Centre square	11
Centre with knock-out pin	12
Centring device	12
Cheap chuck	13
Cheap dividing head	13
Cheaper dust extraction	14
Circular blanks / dovetail chucks	15
Cleaning a face visor	15
Clean screen	15
Concentricity	16
Copying device	16
Coronet spindle-puller	17
Counter production	18
Crosstool holder	18
Cutting abrasive paper	19
Cutting tenons	19

D

De-misting glasses	20
Diameter template	20
Double-ended calliper	20
Dressing grinding wheels	21
Dual-purpose chuck	21
Duckboard for lathe bench	21

E

Extractor selector	22

F

Faceplate fixing	22
Faceplate lever	22
Ferrules for tool handles	23
Filter feature	23
Final sanding	24
Flexi-drill mount	24

G

Get it round	24
Get it taped	25
Gluing circular blanks	25
Grinding angles	26
Grip, not slip	26
Guide lines	26

H

Hand-made chuck	27
Hand thread chasing	28
Handy dust extraction	29
Hold it!	29
Home-made lathe	30

I

Indexing plate	30
Indexing plate for Coronet	31
Is your scalpel askew?	31

J

Jack it up	32

K

Know your square drill	32

L

Lathe faceplates from pulleys	32
Light cord pulls	33
Long small tapers	33
Long toolrest	34

M

Making a bowl steady	34
Mandrel for wheel-making	35
Marking burrs for bowls	35
Measuring idea	36
Mobile bench and lathe	36
Mobile tool stands	36
Modification to older Jubilee lathe	37
Modified compression/expansion chuck	38
Multi-jaws for Multistar	39

N

No more wayward ways	39
Non-slip floor	39

P

Parting saw versus parting chisel	40
Parting tool (1)	40
Parting tool (2)	40
Pin chuck alternative	41
Pocket centre finder	42
Preparing end of spindles	42
Protection from jaws	43

R

Rawlbolt chuck	43
Rear toolrest support	44
Rechucking	44
Recycled brace and bits	45
Roller blind	45
Rotating chisel holder	45

S

Sanding drum	46
Safe faceplate fixing	47
Save polish - and mess	47
Short turnings	48
Simple bowl steady and live centre	48
Soft touch	49
Sore patches salved	49
Space-saver stand	49
Split turnings made easy	50
Stop wandering drills	50
Switchgear solution	51

T

Tailstock centre tray	52
Tool rack (1)	52
Tool rack (2)	53
Tools for a song	53
Trammel gauge for pence	54
Two for the price of one	54
Two-way depth guage	54

U

Un-notchable tool rest	55

W

Waste not...	55
Wooden faceplates	55
Work-holding jig	56

INTRODUCTION

With the phenomenal growth in interest in woodturning over the last few years, it is not surprising that a whole support industry has expanded to meet the demands of the army of new enthusiasts.

We have seen the formation of the Association of Woodturners of Great Britain, and the tremendously successful launch of *Woodturning* magazine, which now circulates the world. GMC Publications has been in the vanguard of supplying a whole new wave of woodturning books and videos.

Then, of course, there are the tools and equipment. A dazzling array of new lathes, chucks, accessories, tools and other gadgets and gizmos has been launched to attract the professionals and hobbyists alike.

Interest in, and sales of, new woodturning equipment has been mushrooming at special exhibitions and shows around the country, and this despite the recession of recent years.

Newcomers to the craft could be excused for being confused by the vast array of tools and equipment to choose from. And those with deep pockets can enjoy the luxury of experimentation with the latest ideas.

We welcome this expansion of goods, and are always pleased to test new products in our Turning World feature in *Woodturning*.

But at the same time we recognise that there are many more hobby woodturners beavering away in their home workshops on limited budgets. A good few may be retired or unemployed.

Whether from pressure of finances or simply because they enjoy the challenge of working out solutions to problems, these are the folk who consistently come up with the bright ideas to "reach the parts that other tools cannot reach."

And this is where our Tips feature has come into its own. From the very first issue of *Woodturning* we have been pleased to publish the ideas of woodturners which have been passed on to help their fellow craftsmen.

Some of the tips are as old as woodturning itself, but perhaps with a new twist. Some are sparklingly original and ingenious. But all will give someone, somewhere just the answer they need to that thorny problem.

I often wonder how many times the words, "Now why didn't I think of that?!" have echoed around countless workshops over the years.

Necessity is the mother of invention, and you can rely on resourceful woodturners to find the answers. Britain is a nation of inventors, and the proof of that can be found in the following pages.

Many have found inspiration from the tips in this booklet, which are drawn from those published in *Woodturning* over the past three years and 20 issues. We hope that you too will find fresh encouragement and motivation to go looking for new ideas to help yourself and others in your chosen craft.

Don't forget to write and tell us about your ideas – you could find them published in *Woodturning* and win a cash prize to boot!

Happy turning.

Nick Hough

Nick Hough, Editor.

1 Bandsaw sharpener

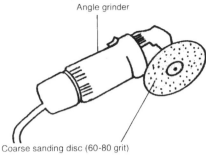

Angle grinder

Coarse sanding disc (60-80 grit)

A quick method to sharpen bandsaw blades *in situ* is to use an anglegrinder fitted with a coarse (usually 60 or 80 grit) sanding disc and to lightly touch the *top* of each tooth with the edge of the disc (see diagram).

Either mark the starting point or, as we do, start and end the sharpening round at the weld site. Normally we get three such 'sharpens' from a blade and the cutting performance is good as the 'set' is unaltered.

The whole task takes just a few minutes, the same time it would take to change a blade. Not for purists, perhaps, but economical and effective.

Ann and Bob Phillips, Acredale, Coastal Highway, Mapua, RD1 Upper Moutere, Nelson, New Zealand.

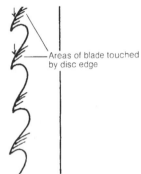

Areas of blade touched by disc edge

Note bandsaw is still on machine at the normal working position

2 Bobbin chuck (1)

Here is a cheap and easy way of making a sturdy 12mm 1/2" bobbin chuck for lathes that take a morse taper.

Cut off the drill section from an old morse taper 6–8mm 1/4"–5/16". Drill size is not critical. Some are to be found already broken off in boot sales or second-hand tool shops.

Now find a 12mm 1/2" bi-hexagon drive socket that is slightly under the drill diameter at the nut end and carefully drive the drill spindle into the socket. If it is a nice tight fit no other fixing is necessary as the star shape of the socket bites into the drill shank.

I found both drill and socket at the same boot sale - price 50p for the two. Since then I have made a 6mm 1/4" and 10mm 3/8" version. All were from the same source and near the same price.

Ray Pearce, 8 Holly Oak Road, Aldermoor, Southampton SO1 6GD.

3 Bobbin chuck (2)

I was interested to read Ray Pearce's letter about making bobbin chucks (Tip 2), but I have my own method.

I make a 10mm 3/8" mortise in the end of a 25mm 1" square piece of hardwood. I then mount

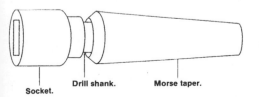

Socket.   **Drill shank.**   **Morse taper.**

7

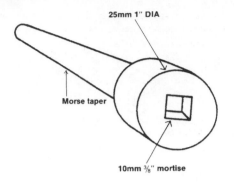

25mm 1" DIA

Morse taper

10mm ⅜" mortise

the pieces between centres, with the revolving tail centre pushed into the square hole, and turn a morse taper to fit my lathe.

It doesn't have to be a perfect taper, but get it as near as you can. It's even cheaper than Ray's idea.

P.A. Symonds, Doublesse House, The Drift, Exning, Newmarket, Suffolk CB8 7EZ.

Bowl design without waste

4

Do you sometimes turn a bowl and find yourself unhappy with the finished shape? It could be because the bowl was not really planned but just 'happened' as you turned it.

It's fine to experiment, but you do not want to waste a really good or expensive piece of wood.

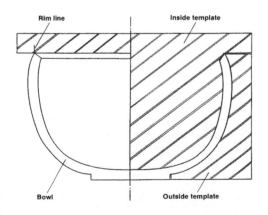

Rim line

Inside template

Bowl

Outside template

Here's an alternative approach to help you plan the shape before you start cutting the wood.

Let's say you start with a good sized blank of 125mm 5" x 200mm 8" DIA. Cut a piece of stout paper (brown wrapping or cartridge) to the size of the maximum cross-section of the disc and fold it in half, short edges together.

Cut the recess for the expanding jaw chuck, or the shape of the base or plinth. Then use scissors (not pencil) to cut out a half profile of pleasing shape. Keep pausing to open out the fold and assess progress. You may be surprised at the fluency of the curves you can produce with scissors as opposed to a pencil.

If you go too far and cut away too much, make a fresh start - it is cheaper than cutting away too much wood.

When you have arrived at an outside shape you like, use it to make a half-profile template in thin plywood or stout card. Then sketch in the inside profile, taking care to get an even thickness in the sides and bottom of the bowl. Now you can make a half-profile template for the inside shape of the bowl.

Using the two templates, and patience, you should be able to transfer the shape to the wood and do justice to the timber.

Peter Baylis, Woodpeckers, 11 Church End, Panfield, Braintree, Essex.

Bullnose centre

5

Bullnose centres are handy for spindle turnings that must be hollowed at one end, such as goblets, cups, vases, etc., but the cost is often prohibitive to the woodturner on a budget.

However, most turners do have an ordinary ball-bearing live centre, for which they can make a simple adaptor to take full advantage of the bullnose centre's features.

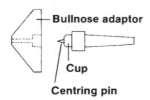

Bullnose adaptor

Cup

Centring pin

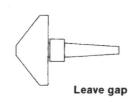

Leave gap

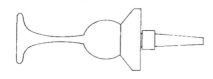

To make the adaptor, glue a block of 75mm x 75mm x 75mm 3" x 3" x 3" maple (or other hard, close-grained wood) to waste stock and mount it on a faceplate with the grain parallel to the turning axis.

Bore a hole for a snug fit around the cup of your live centre. Make the depth of the hole slightly less than the height of the cup, so the adaptor will not bear against the non-rotating part of the live centre.

Bore a second, smaller hole completely through the workpiece. This hole allows room for the centring pin, and provides a means for removing the adaptor from the live centre.

Round the workpiece with a roughing gouge, and then use a skew to cut the taper for the smoothest possible finish. Apply several coats of paste wax to the tapered surface, then part the adaptor from the lathe.

To use the bullnose centre simply press the adaptor onto the live centre cup. The drawing shows how to use it to stabilise a hollowed turning such as a goblet while working the outside.

To separate the bullnose from the live centre, use a piece of metal tubing (such as a section from a telescoping antenna) to tap the live centre out from the narrow end of the bullnose. The tubing's outside diameter should be narrower than the through hole, and the inside diameter should be larger than the centring pin.

Anthony P Matlosz, 8 Arlington Drive, Howell, NJ 07731, USA.

Bumper-outer

Most of us reach for any odd piece of rod to knock out centres from hollow headstock or tailstock. This is not very craftsmanlike and could damage the holes. I made a bumper-outer that does the job better and can take its place alongside the other lathe tools.

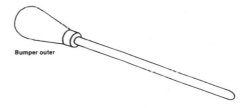

Bumper outer

There is a steel rod that fits loosely in the bore and is more than long enough. Its working end is well rounded. The other end fits in a lumpy wood handle with a brass tube ferrule. It is secured there with epoxy glue (Araldite).

Percy Blandford, Quinton House, Newbold-on-Stour, Stratford-upon-Avon, Warwickshire CV37 8UA.

Centralising gadget

The centralising tool made by A.P.J. Whaley for getting a faceplate duly centred on a blank disc (Tip 8) is a very nice job indeed but, unlike myself, not too many wood-turners will possess a screw-cutting metal lathe. They do not have to seek outside help, however.

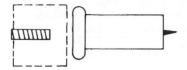

Two years ago I solved the same problem with a simple wooden gadget. Since the spindlenose thread of my home-made wood lathe and faceplates is 3/4" BSP parallel, I turned a short length of beech down to 24mm 15/16" so as to slide smoothly through the faceplate. A 2mm 1/16" hole bored in the end was filled with a suitable nail (with the point cut off before insertion), the exposed end being cut off to 6mm 1/4" and filed to a point while the lathe was turning. A flat knob was turned 50mm 2" from the end and then the tool was cut off.

In use the tool is dropped into the faceplate from the back, held in place by the knob and the combined 'flying saucer' makes a one-point landing on the centre of the turning blank. I hope this information will be of use to some fellow turners.

Rien Blomsma, 3067 NV Rotterdam, Edmond Hellenraadstraat 132.

8 Centralising tool

The tool shown in the photograph is one to enable a faceplate to be centralised on a blank disc once the centre has been marked.

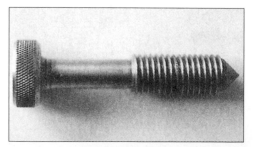

One threads the pointed end through the faceplate from the back, puts the point on the centre mark, rotates the faceplate down until it just touches the wood, attaches the faceplate to wood and removes the tool.

A.P.J. Whaley, 21 Mollatts Close, Ladderedge, Leek, Staffordshire ST13 7AJ.

9 Centre drills

Having taken early retirement after 48 years as a centre turner, I still enjoy turning as a hobby. On reading in your last issue the tip of using a centre drill to minimise splitting (Tip 75), I wish to offer an opposite approach.

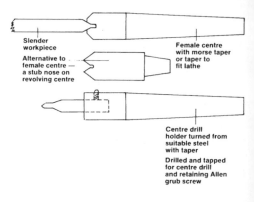

I use a female rear centre which has been drilled with a centre drill instead, as shown in my drawing. Alternatively you can also use a stub nose of a revolving centre. It amazes me that this method has not been adopted before, for clockmakers have used it for countless years.

Another useful idea is to turn a piece of steel which is then drilled and tapped to take a centre drill, the drill being retained with an Allen screw.

S. Ashworth, 1 Richmond Close, Tottington, Bury, Lancs BL8 3HZ.

10 Centre of gravity

It can sometimes be a problem finding the centre for turning a large, odd-shaped burr. I needed to turn a burr 355mm x 230mm 14" x 9" on my Coronet Minor lathe without it walking away.

I remembered from schooldays a method of finding the centre of gravity of an object, and I used it successfully on my burr.

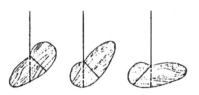

I simply suspended the block with a piece of string at about six different positions and drew vertical lines at each hanging.

This gave me a point on the face side of the burr which I used as the centre point, and I was able to turn the burr with no further problem.

I have since tried this on other odd shapes and it seems to work every time.

P.B. Sawyer, 34 Merynton Avenue, Coventry CV4 7BN.

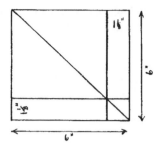

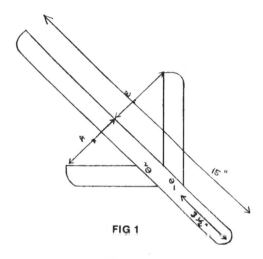

FIG 1

11 Centre square

Spend half-an-hour making a centre square and you will be able to find the centre of any bowl-turning disc up to about 380mm 15" DIA.

An 'L' shape with limbs 30mm 1 1/8" wide is cut from a 150mm 6" square of 10mm 3/8" plywood on which the diagonal has been marked.

A strip of hardwood 380mm 15" x 25mm 1" x

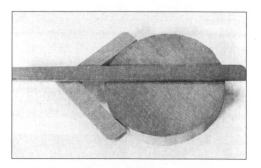

5mm 3/16" is fixed to the diagonal by means of glue and two 12mm 1/2" No 4 countersunk screws.

Screw No 1 in FIG 1 should be inserted first, and measurements A and B checked to be equal before inserting screw No 2.

Round off the corners as shown, drill a hole to hang it up, give it a coat of varnish and you have another useful tool to add to your collection.

The following points should be borne in mind when using the centre square. First, the most accurate results are obtained when the lines drawn across the disc are roughly at right angles to each other.

Second, discs cut from damp or not fully seasoned timber will have shrunk during drying out and, since the greatest shrinkage takes place across the grain, the disc will have become oval in shape. In this case, the lines should be placed as nearly as possible along and across the grain for the best results.

When I showed my centre square to a friend's wife she said it was just the thing for finding the centre and marking out patterns on iced cakes. If you find yourself in a similar position, I suggest perspex would be a better and more hygienic material to use.

Ernest Parrott, 31A Beacontree Avenue, Walthamstow, London E17 4BU.

12 Centre with knock-out pin

You can turn quite fast and never stop the lathe on small objects using this large dead centre with a knock-out centre pin. I made this for turning wooden handles - I must have made thousands.

They fit on a bar handle of 90mm x 32mm 3 1/2" x 1 1/4" finished size. I also use this gadget when making lamp base holes, pepper mills and salt shakers instead of making wooden arbors or jam chucks.

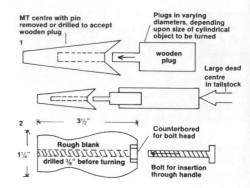

To make a handle I first drill a 10mm 3/8" hole through the rough blank, then counterbore one end to fit the handle bolt. This method works for any cylinder shape. It's a lot quicker and easier as the holes are concentric.

I knock the loose centre pin out of a good sized centre, then I make plugs to replace the centre. I make a lot of different sizes to compensate for the hole.

Lloyd P. Humiston, 25800 Corson, Sun City, CA 92584, USA.

13 Centring device

To find the centre of bowl blanks with a pair of dividers can be time consuming and sometimes not very accurate. A quick and easy tool can be made from a disc of clear perspex or other clear rigid plastic about 255mm 10" dia and 3mm 1/8" thick.

Pierce a small hole in the centre large enough to allow a pencil point through. With a pair of dividers or trammel bar inscribe circles around the centre at regular gaps, say 12mm 1/2". These can be coloured with fine felt tip pens.

To use, lay the disc on to the wooden blank and line up the circumference of the wood within the closest circle, the centre is then easy to mark through the hole. This is also useful when turning end grain wood with contrasting coloured grain such as yew and laburnum for decorative goblets and small bowls as it enables you to see the effect you would get with using different centre positions. The device can also be used when working with irregular shaped wood, as you can see the amount to be turned off before you get a cylindrical form.

John Viggers, 'Flamerty', The Ridgeway, Bloxham, Banbury, Oxon OX15 4NF.

14 Cheap chuck

After reading an article about chucks I thought you would be interested to hear about a mini-lathe I have just made.

I am an engineering machinist and needed a simple chuck to turn very small items.

On acquiring a 2" diameter piece of aluminium, I sawed off two discs. One to suit my lathe thread length and one approx 3/8" wide.

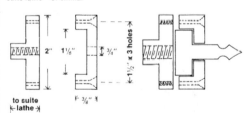

The lathe half was threaded and put onto the lathe. This I machined with H/S steel woodturning tools quite easily. I then drilled and threaded this half 5mm threaded at 1 1/2" centres. I drilled the mating half the same and countersunk it. I then clamped together in lathe and turned bore and recess for my needs.

As the drawing shows, this cheap chuck could be made any size depending upon your own requirements.

G. Mayer, 22 Mayfield Avenue, Newcastle, Staffs ST5 2JR.

15 Cheap dividing head

Here is an idea for a cheap dividing head. You will need two gears, one with even numbered teeth for even divisions and one with odd numbered teeth for odd divisions. This gives you greater variations in the divisions. Gears from a motorcycle would do.

Attach the gears to the outboard side of your headstock shaft. I threaded mine to match the thread on my spindle, but you could clamp or bolt the middle to the spindle.

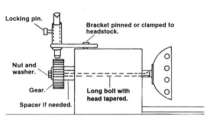

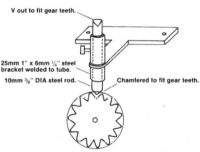

If you have a hollow main spindle, grind the head of a long bolt to a taper and fit it into the morse taper recess of the spindle. Bolt the gear to the other end. On some lathes you may need a spacer bush between the gear and the headstock.

Make a bracket from 25mm 1" x 6mm 1/4" steel and weld on a steel tube and 10mm 3/8" rod. The rod is held in the tube with a locking pin. Chamfer the end of the rod to fit into the gear teeth. This makes a very accurate locking dividing head.

Graham Mayer, 22 Mayfield Avenue, Newcastle, Staffs ST5 2JR.

16 Cheaper dust extraction

Dust extraction is a never-ending problem where lathes are used, and when the by-products of sanders, bandsaws, routers, etc. are added the workshop soon becomes a health and fire hazard.

Amateurs tend to be most at risk as the home workshop does not attract the attention of the health and safety inspectorate and such equipment is not always considered a priority. It is looked upon as a desirable feature rather than a necessity and the financial outlay is very often the deciding factor.

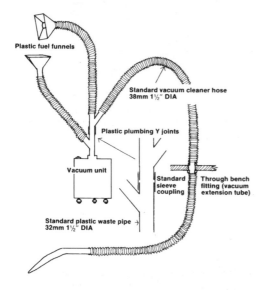

Plastic fuel funnels

Standard vacuum cleaner hose 38mm 1½" DIA

Plastic plumbing Y joints

Vacuum unit

Standard sleeve coupling

Through bench fitting (vacuum extension tube)

Standard plastic waste pipe → 32mm 1½" DIA

My own solution has proved very effective for minimal outlay, and has given me a versatile system.

Obviously the vacuum unit is the main expense but it is possible to acquire a reliable unit, wet/dry type vacuum from auctions, car-boot sales or from dealers as ex-trade-in for £20-£30. A large capacity collection bag is an important feature to look for.

Ordinary vacuum hoses of about 38mm 1 1/2" DIA are ideal as they are readily available and

can be obtained in various lengths. They need not be new and the fittings are not required except for the one that connects to the unit.

I have a three-way extraction system that provides two collectors for the lathe and a wander-hose for general workshop cleaning and connecting to the bandsaw and router bench. I have a sanding machine which is placed in front of the lathe and the lower collector catches virtually all the sanding dust as it comes off the end of the belt.

The photograph shows the two collectors (plastic fuel funnels which push straight into the hose) and the wander-hose which can also clip above the workpiece in the lathe or can be used separately. To increase the vacuum power in any one of the outlets a cone plug or bung is fitted into the other outlets.

The three-way link-up is simply made up of two standard plastic plumbing 'Y' joints connected to make a three-into-one pipeline. These are available in various diameters and the common household waste pipe fittings of 32mm 1 1/4" DIA are an excellent fit into most vacuum hoses.

The result, for a moderate outlay of less than £40, is no blocked sinuses and a cleaner and safer workshop.

John Marshall, Mistral, Clos de Cordage, Le Tertre, Castel, Guernsey, Channel Islands.

17 Circular blanks/dovetail chucks

There is an easier and simpler way of producing circular blanks than that described in the article 'Blankety Blank' in issue no. 4.

Cut a circle out of stout card or hardboard the size of blank required. Nail this on top of the lump of wood to be sawn. The length of the nail is determined by the unevenness of the wood; there is no need to drive the nail home. The blank can now be sawn with the bandsaw blade by following the edge of the card. As long as the card is held within 10° of the horizontal, an accurate disk will be cut with the centre already marked by the nail hole.

On the subject of removing the recess (made for a dovetail chuck) from the base of a bowl, and the elaborate ways suggested for doing this, why start with a dovetail chuck? What is wrong with gluing a blank to a wooden faceplate with stout brown paper between? The layer of brown paper, which sticks to the bowl when it is prised off the faceplate, is easily removed, depending on the glue used!

J.N. Halcrow, 'Vire', Homebank, Coldstream, Berwickshire TD12 4ND.

18 Cleaning a face visor

A method of removing the misting effect of those irritating surface scratches which build up on your face visor.

This tip was given to me by a watch repairer who cleans scratched plastic or perspex watch face covers using a more sophisticated system but employing the same principles as described below.

Method
1. Detach the face visor from the head brace.

2. Place onto a soft cloth on a flat and firm surface.

3. Using a soft cloth, apply a burnishing cream by rubbing in a circular motion over the whole surface of the visor. (I use Liberon and apply it in the same fashion as I would apply polish to the car - if I ever polished it!)

4. Swill off with clean warm water.

5. Polish with a clean, dry cloth.

6. Turn the face visor over and repeat the process on the other side.

Note
In order not to compound the problem, it is important to remember that throughout the cleaning process only soft cloths must be used.

Do not leave the cleaning process until the face mask is badly scratched. Best results are gained by regular cleaning applications.

Serious scratches can be removed by using a more abrasive cream (Jif), followed by burnishing cream. (Using the same principle as for sanding; from coarse grit to fine.)

Each cleaning application will produce better results.

S. Leach, 90 Hunters Way, Penkhull, Stoke-on-Trent ST4 5EF.

19 Clean screen

I do a lot of wet turning and use a full face visor and helmet. I have experienced problems with sap and resin spraying on to the visor. If allowed to dry it becomes difficult to remove and in the removing there is a risk of damage to the surface of the visor. Visor replacement then is required at fairly short intervals.

I have solved this problem by covering the outside face of the visor with a layer of kitchen cling-film (alas, more cadging of the wife's kitchen materials). After a session of roughing out wet bowls, I simply peel off the cover of cling-film and replace with a clean piece.

Although there is a slight impairment of vision, it has no effect at the rough turning stage.

I am a regular reader of your magazine and I must congratulate you on a very informative and well-balanced periodical.

Austin McNally, 31 Manse Road, Carrowdore, Co Down, Northern Ireland BT22 2EZ.

A more sophisticated version of this method is used by Formula 1 racing drivers to keep their visors clear, but we think this home-made version should work equally well. - Ed.

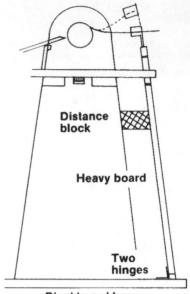

End View **Preferred height**

Distance block

Heavy board

Two hinges

Blockboard base

20 Concentricity

When you turn a piece between centres using a two-pronged centre, you sometimes need to remove it for some reason. However, if you do not replace it on the prongs in exactly the same way as before you lose concentricity.

My tip is to put a dab of red paint on the side of one of the prongs, and mark the workpiece with a pencil by the indentation made by this prong. You will then always be sure to remount the piece in exactly the same way and maintain concentricity.

H. Lance Beausire, 1 Rue Lechevallier, 76310 Sainte-Adresse, France.

21 Copying device

I have devised this copying device very cheaply using some boards and some flexible rods, which are the bristles from an industrial road sweeper. The bristles are 255mm 10" long by about 1mm 1/16" dia. They are preset to the shape of the required article and, when offered to the blank bend upwards. No doubt you could use other suitable materials for the flexible rods.

This is like a giant version of commercially available shape tracers, but with my idea the bristles are in contact with the workpiece right up to the point where the required profile is achieved. A shape tracer can be offered to the workpiece only when it has stopped turning and will only fit the turned piece when all the cuts have been made.

My design means that the flexible bristles will return to their original straight form when the piece being turned reaches the correct diameter. Because the bristles are thin the device will allow the turner to duplicate jobs with intricate shapes. The number of bristles used will be determined by the number of changes of shape required, and the device can be made of any length to suit.

I have mounted my device using hinges so it can be swung away from the lathe when not in use. The distancing block is important and adds stability.

I have indicated two suggested heights for the device - use the one where it is easiest for you to

Holding down screws

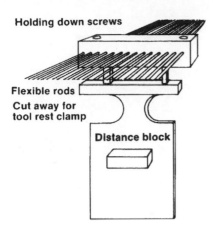

Flexible rods

Cut away for tool rest clamp

Distance block

View from above

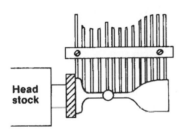

Head stock

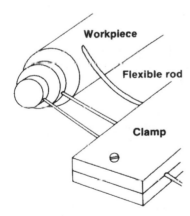

Workpiece

Flexible rod

Clamp

see exactly when the bristles have returned to their original straight shape. When you are setting it up make sure that the bristles are pointing to the centre of the workpiece.

Michael Pickard, 60 Newman Road, Grange Estate, Whiston, Rotherham S60 3JD.

22 Coronet spindle-puller

When I needed to change the drive belt on my Coronet No 1 lathe, the instruction manual suggested using a hammer and brass or copper drift to knock out the spindle. I thought it would be better to make a puller.

I made one very simply using a 63mm 2 1/2" length of 50mm 2" DIA metal pipe, a 6mm 1/4" thick steel plate and a 10mm 3/8" bolt and nut (see drawing).

You simply unscrew the thread protector, drop the countersunk bolt through, screw the protector back on the spindle, position the pipe, and put the plate over the bolt with the washer and nut. With the M6 screw taken out from the tail end of the spindle, tightening the nut will easily draw out the spindle.

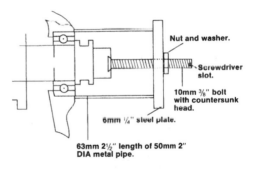

Nut and washer.

Screwdriver slot.

10mm ⅜" bolt with countersunk head.

6mm ¼" steel plate.

63mm 2½" length of 50mm 2" DIA metal pipe.

Once the drive belt has been changed, relocating the spindle is made much easier by screwing a length of 6mm studding in the tail end. With a large washer and nut you can draw the spindle back into position with only a light tap with a piece of wood on the thread protector.

M. Pavey, 1 North Close, Draycott, Cheddar, Somerset BS27 3TY.

23 Counter production

Here is a method I devised when I had to turn a large number of ash discs or counters for use in board games. I started with 38mm 1 1/2" square ash cut into 305mm 12" lengths and turned and sanded these to finished diameter (31mm 1 3/16").

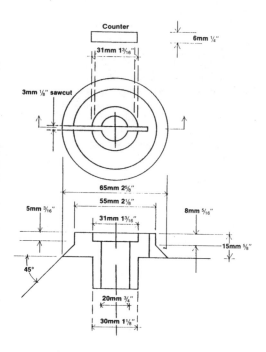

Section through collet to fit Myford chuck

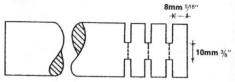

faced to the correct thickness and a surface decoration/pattern applied.

If you were producing enough counters it could be worthwhile to make a complete form/facing tool.

Reg Long, Brooklea, Ford, Chippenham SN14 8RR.

24 Crosstool holder

Here are some drawings of a crosstool holder I use on my lathe for deep bowl turning. Others might find this idea useful too.

I have a rather massive lathe with a 6" x 3" iron bed, 10' long, so I don't have many problems. As I do a lot of faceplate turning, for convenience I devised a tool post holder to go across the lathe bed to which the tool rest is attached.

As you can see from the drawing the construction is quite straightforward. Dimensions are not given, for these will vary with the lathe in your possession.

Using this crosstool holder I find that I can cut the

Next I used a thin parting tool to part down to 10mm 3/8" DIA at 8mm 5/16" intervals along each cylinder. This ensured enough wood was left to finish the counters to the required thickness (6mm 1/4").

The counters were then quickly cut off on the bandsaw by cutting through the 10mm 3/8" spigots.

I next turned a collet from well-seasoned boxwood to fit the Myford combination chuck on my Myford ML8 lathe. This enabled me to grip each counter so both sides could quickly be

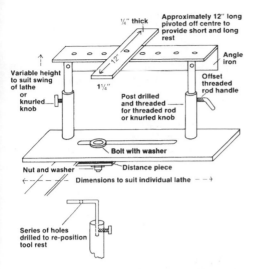

bottom and sides of a bowl much more easily. This method is like the old bodger's board or stick and I find this the best way.

Lloyd P. Humiston, 25800 Corson, Sun City, CA 92584, USA.

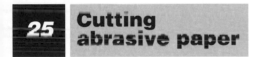

25 Cutting abrasive paper

Having for some time torn sheets of abrasive paper in half by folding them and hoping the tear would follow the fold, which it never does, thus wasting abrasive paper, I made the appliance shown here from a scrap of ply, a worn 305mm 12" hacksaw blade and a mahogany offcut.

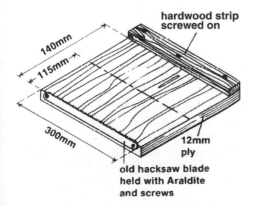

hardwood strip screwed on

140mm

115mm

300mm

12mm ply

old hacksaw blade held with Araldite and screws

The sketch is self explanatory. The hacksaw blade has the set ground off so that each tooth is a sharp point. In use, the paper is pushed against the stop, held down flat with one hand and torn by pulling it down across the blade with the other hand. As I often use a quarter of a sheet, I scribed a line on the board to line the paper up for the second tier.

Jim Kingshott, Heatherbrae Workshop, Woodend Road, Deepcut, Nr Camberley, Surrey GU16 6QH.

26 Cutting tenons

There are many small things that can help us to do better work. Using an open wrench to cut tenons on spindles has been very helpful to me.

I grind a sharp edge on the short side of the wrench with a small bevel on the inside. The tenon is then cut to about 3mm 1/8" oversize with a parting tool.

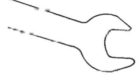

To finish the tenon, hook the unsharpened end under the oversize tenon and push the sharp edge into the wood. Repeat this across the length of the tenon.

The inside bevel cuts a bit oversize, so, after you have finished cutting, push the wrench all of the way onto the tenon and slide it back and forth. This will compress the wood down to the size of the wrench.

Wrenches are a bit larger than the size indicated so an oversize drill should be used for making the holes. The moisture in the glue will cause the compressed wood to expand to make a good tight fit. If an exact-size tenon is necessary, grind the next smaller size wrench to the exact size.

My history covers 50 years of professional carpenter and hobbyist wood worker, woodcarver and wood turner.

Norris White, 204 Farmers Lane, Sellersville, PA 18960-1544, USA.

27 De-misting glasses

One of the most annoying problems I suffered as a relatively new hobby woodturner was the fogging of spectacles while turning with paper mask and safety glasses on.

The reason - I think - for fogging is the temperature differential between the warm air exhaled and the colder lens.

With this in mind, and because I turn with the aid of a spotlight in a smallish workshop, I now heat my spectacles and safety glasses on the spotlight for 15 minutes before starting to turn. This works well.

Dennis Barrow, 15 Caribbean Crescent, Happy Valley 5159, South Australia.

28 Diameter template

When turning one or several specific diameters (particularly on a number of similar pieces), instead of having to constantly check the diameter(s) with a calliper a simple method is to use a pre-fabricated template in Formica.

For instance, you require to constantly check diameters of 20mm 3/4" one end and 30mm 1 1/8" the other. Bore holes of both diameters in a scrap of Formica and saw these accurately through the centres into two halves. This will give you your template (two in fact - so you'll have a spare!).

On a small piece of Formica say 14cm long by 6cm wide you can drill holes to say 10, 12, 14, 16, 18 and 20mm on one side and 22, 24, 26 and 28mm on the other, all the centres on each side being on the same line through which the saw cut is made.

I also have one such template for my 6-in-1 chuck which requires diameters of 43 1/2, 35 1/2 and 30mm (and 2 1/2") for the split rings. I find this very useful (copy herewith).

If drill bits are not available for the diameters required simply inscribe circles with a pair of dividers and cut out the semi-circles with a fine fretsaw. It is as well to clearly mark the half circles produced with the corresponding diameter.

H.Lance Beausire, 1 Rue Lechevallier, 76310 Sainte-Adresse, France.

29 Double-ended calliper

A double-ended calliper is useful when turning bowls and vessels if you need an accurate measurement of wall thickness.

I made my own from a piece of 2mm thick aluminium. I cut out the sections with a jigsaw and metal-cutting blade. It is fixed at the centre with a small nut, bolt and washers, with a split spring washer between the two parts.

Having one leg straight and one curved means you can get into narrow opening vessels. Mine is 400mm 16" x 100mm 4" but you can of course make any size.

P.A. Symonds, Doublesse House, The Drift, Exning, Newmarket, Suffolk CB8 7EZ.

30 Dressing grinding wheels

Not everyone has money for grinding wheel dressers! I find that, with suitable eye protection, you can quite easily straighten the wheel with a masonry bit. By guiding it squarely across the wheel, the tungsten will quickly dress the wheel.

L.J. Jackson, 28 Nant Hall Road, Prestatyn, Clwyd LL19 9LN.

31 Dual-purpose chuck

This idea is for converting a standard 12mm 1/2" drill chuck to give you a dual-purpose drive centre. The chuck is fitted to a morse taper arbor suited to your lathe headstock.

If you grind the three jaws to the shape shown, a solid three-prong driving dog is made (Photo 1). This can further be used to grip a centre pin of the appropriate size to suit the job in hand (Photo 2).

Photo 1 Three-prong driving dog

Photo 2 Pin chuck centre

Centre pins can be made from silver steel and may be hardened and tempered if necessary. They must be long enough to bottom in the chuck body when gripped in the jaws so they do not push back in use.

The pin lengths decrease as the diameters increase. Pins ranging from 2mm 3/32" to 10mm 3/8" DIA will cover most between centre turnings, from miniature to quite large.

Even if you buy a new chuck it is still cheaper than two drive centres, and you still have a perfectly good drill chuck. Of course care will be needed when reverting to normal chuck use as the jaws are sharp and could damage wood being drilled.

Reg Long, Brooklea, Ford, Chippenham SN14 8RR.

32 Duckboard for lathe bench

Having made a duckboard for my lathe bench I then hinged it to the legs as shown in the diagram. In the upright position, it is easy to sweep up shavings and, in my case, is out of the way of my car. The advantages of a duckboard: Keeps your feet warm in winter and dry if a stream flows through the workshop. For shorter people, or 'authorised children' in the family, permits a more comfortable working height when turning.

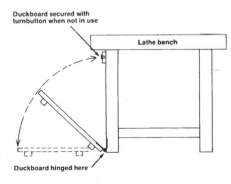

Duckboard secured with turnbutton when not in use

Lathe bench

Duckboard hinged here

S. Ashby, 43 Attwood Crescent, Wyken, Coventry CV2 3JY.

33 Extractor selector

I made this device so I could have my dust extractor connected to whichever machine I was using. I have used just two holes and hoses, for my bandsaw and lathe, but you could of course have any number by enlarging the base.

The base board and top board are made of MDF because it is flat, heavy and makes a good seal. The extractor and machines are connected by means of standard 100mm 4" flexible plastic plumbing pipe.

The top board has to be moved just 125mm 5" for a full changeover from one hole to the other (100mm 4" hole plus 25mm 1" gap between). The rear batten is screwed to the wall and the front supported on legs for extra stability.

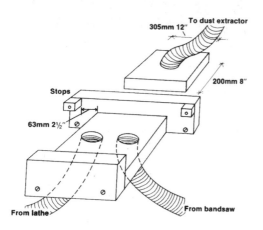

Some people simply bung the ends of spare hoses they are not using, but my device is more efficient. Also, I could not bung the hose going to the bandsaw because the dust extractor outlet hole on it is partly blocked by a pulley.

The top and bottom pieces measure 305mm 12" x 200mm 8" and the rear batten is 485mm 19" long which allows the top 63mm 2 1/2" travel either side between the 25mm 1" square stops.

Neville Tunmore, 44 Shrub Lane, Burwash, East Sussex TN19 7BU.

34 Faceplate fixing

How do you fix your workpiece to your faceplate when it is not possible to use screws? May I pass on a way that is simple and time-saving.

Cut out a wooden disc to fit your faceplate in 12mm 1/2" thick wood. Screw it firmly on the faceplate. Put it on the lathe and score the face of it every 12mm 1/2" with the parting tool about 1/8" deep ... to make a tread. Take off the disc and cut a channel from side to side through the centre, say 10mm 3/8" wide and 6mm 1/4" deep.

On to this is stuck double-sided carpet tape which is best purchased from a carpet factor because it is stronger and wider than that sold by DIY shops. Stick the tape onto the faceplate first and then the workpiece onto that, with care as to centring. It makes assurance doubly sure if the faceplate and workpiece are clamped together in the carpenter's vice. If the vice won't hold them all at once, turn through 180° after ten or 15 minutes.

When lifting off the work from the faceplate, insert a screwdriver or chisel in the channel you have cut in the faceplate and TWIST, at least at the start. Adhesion is very strong and it is possible to fracture work by initial levering.

The size of job can easily embrace a 150mm 6" or more platter or bowl and the device is very useful for turning ordinary flat bottomed jobs like wine bottle coasters and ash trays. A great time saver too.

H.A. Sawyer, 'Thatches', Staplehay, Taunton TA3 7HB.

35 Faceplate lever

After much heavy turning a faceplate can become very tight on the thread of the mandrel nose. I use a lever to free it. This is a long piece of hardwood about 25mm 1" by 12mm 1/2" section

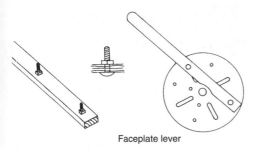

Faceplate lever

with two coach bolts of a diameter to fit easily into the holes of the faceplate.

Instead of making the lever to fit across the diameter of the faceplate, it is arranged off-centre so it can be used on the back of the faceplate when a bowl or other turning is still attached to it. For some faceplates there may have to be a hollow in one edge of the wood to fit around the boss of the faceplate.

Percy W. Blandford, Quinton House, Newbold-on-Stour, Stratford-upon-Avon, Warwickshire CV37 8UA.

 36 **Ferrules for tool handles**

To get a nice fit, on the handle, cut ferrules with a crimp on one end. I use brass tubing or brass water pipe. First mark the ferrule lengths on the pipe. Cut the first mark with a tubing cutter, the next mark with a saw, then alternate with the tubing cutter and saw. This makes ferrules with one end crimped and the other end open (open end goes on the handle first).

K. Gerald Brown, PO Box 566, Tijeras, NM 87059, USA.

Andrew Peterson, Westview Cottage, West End, Stainforth, Doncaster, South Yorkshire DN7 5SA.

37 **Filter feature**

My lathe has a common 3/4" x 16 metric thread on the headstock. While servicing my car, I noticed that the oil filter had the same sized thread, and I found it fitted perfectly on my lathe.

I cut off the outer casing of the filter with a hacksaw as close to the threaded end as I could, just behind the rim. I then used an old file to remove the burr.

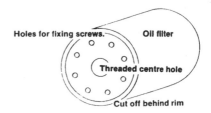

Holes for fixing screws. Oil filter
Threaded centre hole
Cut off behind rim

The faceplate can be attached to a suitable blank of hardwood and used to make a screw chuck, by centre drilling from the tailstock, and entering a suitable sized screw into the drilled pilot hole. Remove the head and unthreaded part of the screw with a hacksaw

You could also attach a piece of hardwood, then screw through from the rear with long screws into the workpiece, drilling pilot holes in line with the holes in the faceplate.

A third method is to centre a large steel nut on the lathe. Using the tailstock and a Jacobs chuck, hold the nut against the faceplate, and weld it in position. This makes a threaded cup chuck.

To use as a cup chuck, turn a spindle of wood between centres, with a spigot to fit tight into the nut on the drive end of the job. This is ideal for making handles, and enabling tailstock drilling to be done in timber while unsupported. A hole can be drilled into the side of the nut, allowing a wood screw to be used to help hold the wood.

Of course, different filters have different size threads. If your lathe is not of this size, inquire at any motorists' store or garage to see if a suitable filter is available.

38 Final sanding

Sometimes after finishing a piece of work you become aware of small rough sections left in internal corners that are difficult to reach.

My solution is to use an old-fashioned two-prong clothes peg with one prong cut off. I wrap abrasive paper round the other prong, attaching it with double-sided sticky tape.

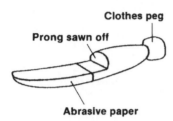

Clothes peg
Prong sawn off
Abrasive paper

This gives you a shape which is flat on one side and rounded on the other - ideal for reaching into most corners - and with a ready-made handle.

Another idea for reaching flat areas in tight situations is to use an old metal nail file bent to the required shape.

Roy Colbourne, 74 Manor House Lane, Yardley, Birmingham B26 1PR.

39 Flexi-drill mount

A flexible drive powered by an electric drill is useful for sanding on the lathe. But when the drill is mounted on the bench, unnecessary strain can be put on the flexible drive when sanding at some angles.

This idea allows the drill a certain amount of movement during the sanding.

Take a piece of 25mm 1" x 25mm 1" wood slightly longer than your drill and screw an eye ring into each end. Tape the wood along the top

of the drill, taking care not to block any air holes. Next, fix two more eye rings to an overhead beam. Take two elastic luggage straps and hook them into the eye rings, hooking the drill eyes on to the other end, so the drill is suspended on the luggage straps.

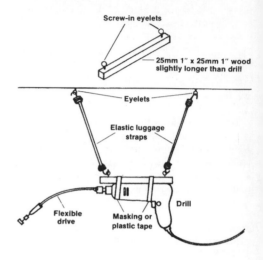

Screw-in eyelets
25mm 1" x 25mm 1" wood slightly longer than drill
Eyelets
Elastic luggage straps
Drill
Flexible drive
Masking or plastic tape

The eyes in the overhead beam should be wider spaced than those on the drill to reduce the risk of the drill twisting under torque if excessive pressure is put on the sanding pad.

I have found the ideal height of the drill to be about waist level. I also use a power file one-handed while sanding small, hand-held articles. A single elastic luggage strap supports the weight of the power file, at about chest level.

Michael Corsby, 2 Sheepcote, Denston, Newmarket, Suffolk CB8 8PN.

40 Get it round

When turning bowls using a dovetail jaw chuck it is very annoying to find, when the blank has been turned on the outside and reversed onto the chuck for turning out the inside, that concentricity has been lost. I am sure this causes the loss of many a valuable bowl blank.

If this loss of concentricity has not been caused by the jaws having been strained or a piece of unnoticed debris getting stuck in the recess prior to mounting, it may have been caused by slight warping of the bottom of the recess.

Find the high point on the bowl rim by revolving over the banjo or a piece of wood laid on the banjo until it rubs. Mark this point on the rim, then take the bowl off the chuck and put a slip of worn abrasive into the recess on this side. A few minutes' trial and error will find the thickness required to get the bowl running concentrically.

R.W. Fernie, Gourdiemuir, Glenfoot, Abernethy, Perthshire PH2 9LS, Scotland.

 # Get it taped

When you are turning a very thin-walled bowl you sometimes get trouble with chatter and vibrations and it is difficult to get a clean inside cut.

This is my solution. First turn and finish the outside of the bowl. Then wrap some strong tape round the outside rim and down the sides before turning the inside. The tape stabilises the piece and avoids irritating chatter, making the finishing cut much easier to do.

Gora Satterstrom, Fasanstigen 30, 370 24 Nattraby, Sweden.

Choose your tape carefully (e.g. masking tape) and remove it immediately afterwards so as not to strip off the finished surface. - Ed.

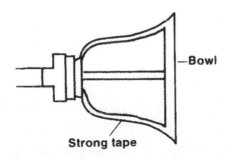

42 Gluing circular blanks

When gluing several pieces of wood together the pieces tend to slide horizontally when pressure is applied. A simple method of avoiding this is shown in the diagram.

Small holes are drilled at or near the centres of the pieces and glue applied. A thin steel rigid rod or wire is inserted and pressure applied with two or more G-clamps, with small pieces of hardboard between them and the wood to prevent marking the latter.

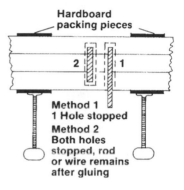

When the glue has set, the rod is easily extricated. For my purposes, I have found this method most successful, as I require the hole in the top to be enlarged with a drill. If desired, however, the hole can be filled and the whole reversed so that the top now becomes the bottom. For some purposes holes can be stopped in both the top and bottom pieces and a shorter rod used, which then remains in the wood.

I have found this method very useful in gluing circular blanks together!

W.M. Ashton, Coed-y-Brain, Antaron Avenue, South Gate, Aberystwyth, Dyfed SY23 1SF.

43 Grinding angles

Setting the toolrest on a bench grinder to the correct angle for a particular gouge, chisel or scraper can be time consuming, especially if over a period of time you've lost the correct angle for the tool or are frequently sharpening different tools.

Here is my solution. Cut some 6mm 1/4" thick wood into strips about 75mm 3" long x 20mm 3/4" wide (the same width as the grinding wheel). Use a joiner's bevel or gauge to mark the required angles on the sides of the strips (FIG 1), then cut them accurately to the correct angle. Check the angles for accuracy with the bevel.

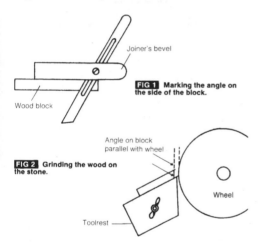

Joiner's bevel

FIG 1 Marking the angle on the side of the block.

Wood block

Angle on block parallel with wheel

FIG 2 Grinding the wood on the stone.

Wheel

Toolrest

You could also get the correct shape by setting the bench grinder toolrest to the appropriate height, so the edge of the wheel is parallel to the drawn line, and grinding the wood away on the coarse stone (FIG 2). (This could clog the wheel.)

Mark the angle on each block and keep the set in a tin near the grinder. When a tool needs sharpening, you simply select the appropriate block, place it on the grinder toolrest and adjust the rest to the correct height by sighting through from the side.

V.C. Hope, 29 Chaddlewood Avenue, Lipson, Plymouth, Devon PL4 8RF.

44 Grip, not slip

Home-made wooden jam chucks have to be accurately turned if the item they are holding is not to slip, if too loose, or be marked if jammed in too tight. I overcome this by using a slightly oversize cup chuck and putting a generous strip of glue round the inside rim with an electric glue gun. The molten glue is rather like toothpaste and can be put on as thickly as required.

It does not matter if the glue is uneven, because when the glue has set you turn the chuck on the lathe and friction melt the glue with a damp cloth pad. This results in a smooth even surface which can be built up to quite a thickness. When the glue has cooled and set, smooth and trim it to the required diameter using a small gouge.

The set glue is semi-soft with some give so it makes a perfect fit and grip on the item to be turned without marking it. By building up or turning down the glue thickness, items of differing diameters can be turned using the same chuck.

No doubt this method could be used on any other wooden chucking system where a good grip is needed without risk of marking the turned item.

S. Leach, 90 Hunters Way, Penkhull, Stoke on Trent ST4 5EF.

45 Guide lines

Here is a useful idea which can be used with an indexing plate of some kind.

You place the 'Wolfcraft' clamp on top of the pedestal with either a drill or a router clamped in it.

The guide pieces reaching between the bed rails will ensure it is centralised either at top dead centre or on the centreline of the lathe.

By turning the workpiece one index point at a time an appropriate edge or centre pattern can be

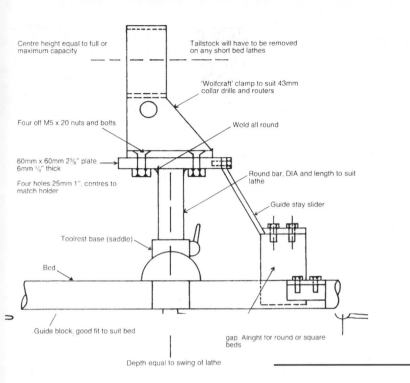

Centre height equal to full or maximum capacity

Tailstock will have to be removed on any short bed lathes

'Wolfcraft' clamp to suit 43mm collar drills and routers

Four off M5 x 20 nuts and bolts

Weld all round

60mm x 60mm 2³/₈" plate. 6mm ¼" thick

Round bar. DIA and length to suit lathe

Four holes 25mm 1", centres to match holder

Guide stay slider

Toolrest base (saddle)

Bed

Guide block, good fit to suit bed

gap. Alright for round or square beds

Depth equal to swing of lathe

made. Alternatively, without the indexing plate the piece can be turned by hand while the drill/router is cutting the desired pattern.

The use of the router opens it up to lots of possibilities with bowl and plate work and, I dare say, goblets.

D.G. Ribbons, 388 Leymoor Road, Golcar, Huddersfield, West Yorkshire HD7 4QF.

46 Hand-made chuck

The first issue of *Woodturning* is very good.

I have been turning wood since I was 16 years old - over 80 now, still turning.

I started making handles and spools for 1 1/2–2 pence a piece. Most of the chucks and mandrels I use are hand-made to quicken the progress.

E. Conover's jam chuck is all right but limited. I have wooden chucks that will fit any geometric figure that can be drawn of a circle. I make a lot of wooden boxes, jewelry, covers for jam and coffee jars, etc. A sample lid is enclosed. Keep it, it fits most coffee jars and makes a nice Christmas gift when filled up with sweets and a ribbon.

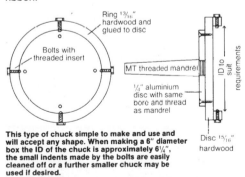

Ring ¹³/₁₆" hardwood and glued to disc

Bolts with threaded insert

MT threaded mandrel

ID to suit requirements

¼" aluminium disc with same bore and thread as mandrel

Disc ¹⁵/₁₆" hardwood

This type of chuck simple to make and use and will accept any shape. When making a 6" diameter box the ID of the chuck is approximately 6¼", the small indents made by the bolts are easily cleaned off or a further smaller chuck may be used if desired.

I am enclosing a rough sketch of a chuck I use a lot. If interested, I have more. I'll take some pictures and send them.

The type of chuck illustrated will fit from a tight fit to 1/2" smaller. You can see how simple it is and quicker. It will fit and hold any geometric figure. I make the chuck from 13/16" stock.

If I make a 6" box, I make the ID of the chuck about 6 1/4" diameter. The small indents can easily sand off. Or I have another chuck to turn them in round. All fit on this centre. It screws on and off quickly.

Lloyd P. Humiston, 25800 Corson, Sun City, CA 92355, USA.

47 Hand thread chasing

Chasing screw threads by hand can cause problems as it seems to be an art that can only be learnt by practice and experience. I have found, however, it is a help if you have some idea of the speed needed to slide the chaser along the rest to engage the work and produce a good thread.

Even those who use a sort of rounding action of the chaser to strike a thread I'm sure would benefit from this.

My solution to enable me to achieve the correct speed of approach is to fix one end of a piece of studding (the same TPI as the thread to be cut) to the centre of the work to be threaded while the other end of the studding is centred and located on the tailstock centre.

A piece of wood or the chaser is pressed against the studding while both work and studding are rotating in unison. This will cause the piece of wood or the chaser to traverse along the toolrest at the correct speed (FIG 1).

The wood needs to be run up and down a number of times to form a thread in the wood. This has the added advantage that you are getting extra practice and not cutting the studding which is likely to happen if you use the chaser.

The studding may be fixed to the workpiece either by using a tapped hole, or more conveniently by pointing the end of the studding and filing a chisel edge like a flatbit drill.

This chisel edge end is pressed, by screwing in the tailstock centre, into a small centre hole drilled or turned in the end of the work. Surprisingly this holds quite well even in the end of a brass workpiece.

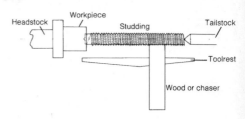

FIG 1 Using studding as a guide.

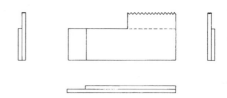

FIG 2 Two pieces of wood glued together to make an L.

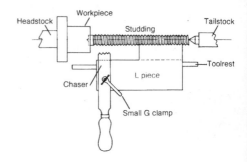

FIG 3 Using the L piece to cut the thread.

This idea led me to devising other ways of cutting threads which are not strictly hand chasing. For example, using an arm with a threaded hole, the same TPI as the screw you wish to cut. The arm has a small slide with a single point threading tool. The arm is traversed along the toolrest by a screw similarly fixed to the work as the studding mentioned above.

The small slide allows the single point threading tool to be advanced into the work, and retracted when reversing the rotation of the work together with the screw. Obviously this can only be done on a slow-speed lathe with reverse rotation facility.

An even more sophisticated arrangement had a rotating cutter instead of the single point tool, but in this instance the work has to be rotated very slowly.

My solution to these two methods is rather crude, and is simply two pieces of wood glued together in the form of a letter L. The longer side of the L has the chaser clamped to it with a small G clamp. The shorter side of the L is pressed into the studding as described previously (FIGS 2 and 3).

The longer the length of engagement with the studding the better. The chaser is moved along the rebate until it is in the position to lightly cut a thread on the work, then it is clamped by a small G clamp.

It is now only a question of making sure to keep the short side of the L pressed against the studding and then release when sufficient length of thread has been cut.

You can continue altering the position of the chaser to cut the thread deeper, but it is essential to keep the chaser against the rebate when altering the depth of cut.

As this is rather tedious I think it is quite sufficient to cut just a shallow thread by this method, then finish off with the hand chaser on its own. If you intend using this last method then it is advantageous to slightly angle (cant) the chaser, by packing between chaser and rebate, to give a lead in for the chaser.

Derek Pearce, 170 Green Lane, Shepperton, Middlesex TW17 8DZ.

48 Handy dust extraction

I have a small (11' x 5') workshop and wanted to remove as much dust as possible without spending vast sums of money.

Like others before me, I used a wet and dry vacuum cleaner as the basis for my system. It has good capacity and better than average suction for a domestic machine.

It is housed in a small shed next to my workshop so dust cannot get back in, and the noise level is kept down. Ducting is the standard 50mm 2" pipe supplied with the machine, which comes through a hole in the wall.

My next idea was to design a user-friendly system for mounting the collector, which is simply the large suction foot attachment supplied with the vacuum.

I did not have enough machines to need multiple collection points, but I wanted the collector to be mobile so I could position it over whichever machine I was using.

I bought an old Anglepoise lamp from a car boot sale for 50p and adapted it to hold the pipe. I then drilled a number of 12mm 1/2" holes near the machines to hold the lamp pivot. You could also use clamps.

Because of the balance mechanism of the lamp, I can now position the collector simply and accurately just where I want it to collect the maximum amount of dust and shavings.

Neil Poston, 46 Littel Tweed, Chelmsford, Essex CM2 6SH.

49 Hold it!

As most of my woodturning is incidental to my other woodwork, I have not considered it worthwhile to buy an expensive metal chuck and accessories, preferring instead to make up my

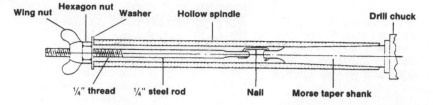

Wing nut · Hexagon nut · Washer · Hollow spindle · Drill chuck

¼" thread · ¼" steel rod · Nail · Morse taper shank

own devices for holding work in the lathe headstock as I need them.

This device is for holding a drill chuck on a morse taper shank so I can use it as a three-jaw chuck for turning small items.

The morse taper shank is held in the hollow headstock spindle by a length of 6mm 1/4" DIA mild steel rod, connected to the shank with a bent nail.

The rod is the type sold by model shops for axles. It is threaded at the end and held in place with a nut and washer. Take care not to overtighten the nut or you will unbend the nail. When the nut is tightened a wing nut locks it securely.

N. Falkiner, 4 Willis Avenue, North Baddesley, Southampton SO52 9EN.

50 Home-made lathe

I do my turning on a home-made gadget which I clamp to the bench with G clamps and power with an old electric motor from an old washing-machine. It suits my purpose just fine.

The photographs illustrate the set-up. The

headstock is a workhead. The tailstock is an old bed bolt with barrel nut rigged up in a wooden bracket with a lock nut at the end. The head was cut off and ground to a 60 point. The washing-machine motor is at rear.

The workhead has a hollow mandrel into which the faceplate, screw chuck and / or driving spur can be fixed. The latter was made from a 1/2" bolt the head of which was cut and filed by hand.

W. Cyril Brown, 22 Kirk Road, Point Lonsdale, Victoria 3225, Australia.

51 Indexing plate

I have a Record Power RPML 300 lathe and sometimes I need to do some indexing work for fluting spindles and decorating a bowl.

The diagram shows the method I use. The spindle thread is 20mm 3/4" TPI, but this can be modified to suit any lathe.

The indexing plate is screwed on to the spindle, followed by the faceplate. The whole locks up and the workpiece can be turned by hand to each position, which is locked by the pin.

For safety, the indexing plate must only be used with the lathe switched off and unplugged. The workpiece is turned by hand.

D.G. Ribbons, 388 Leymoor Road, Golcar, Huddersfield, West Yorkshire HD7 4QF.

INDEXING PLATE
(Tip 51)

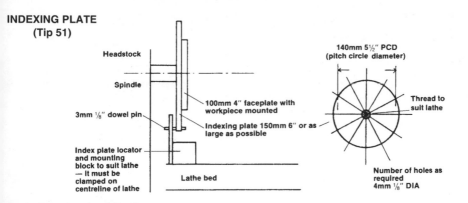

Headstock

Spindle

3mm ⅛" dowel pin

100mm 4" faceplate with workpiece mounted

Indexing plate 150mm 6" or as large as possible

Index plate locator and mounting block to suit lathe — It must be clamped on centreline of lathe

Lathe bed

140mm 5½" PCD (pitch circle diameter)

Thread to suit lathe

Number of holes as required 4mm ⅛" DIA

52 Indexing plate for Coronet

Being unable to find a commercially produced indexing plate for my new Coronet No 3 lathe I got a metal-working friend to make me one. Here's how to make your own.

Remove the screw at the outer end of the main bearing shaft. Make a 70mm 2 3/4" DIA wheel with equally spaced holes on the outer edge - mine has 30 - and screw the wheel into the end of the shaft using the existing screw and washer. Fix a bracket on to the motor clamping lever bolt with a twist in the bracket so the flat face faces the drilled wheel.

Indexing unit for Coronet No 3

Existing screw into existing thread

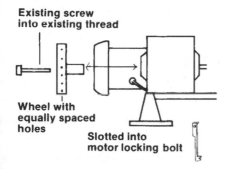

Wheel with equally spaced holes

Slotted into motor locking bolt

Drill a hole through the bracket at the level of the centre of the wheel and fit a screw in the hole so it will fit into any hole on the wheel as it comes level.

This device works admirably. The bracket is removed when using the lathe but the drilled wheel can stay in place.

H.C. Crutchley, Bavaria House, Victoria Road, Aldeburgh, Suffolk IP15 5EF.

53 Is your scalpel askew?

For the best turner's cover-up yet, from neck to mid calf, in stylish green, slip into a Surgeon's Operating Theatre Gown. Very important to ask for the type used by orthopaedic surgeons. This fastens at the back with a generous overlap and also has comfortable knitted cuffs. Made in lightweight non-static close-weave cotton, intended for the steriliser, it tubs easily and dries in a flash.

The purchasing department of your local hospital will tell you the name of their favoured supplier, if you ask them nicely. I get mine from Kinloch Textiles Ltd, Hallam Street, Stockport, Cheshire SK2 6PT. Price about £8.50 including post and VAT, small, medium and large sizes. At half the price of the usual turner's smock, it's a real bargain.

Bill Kinsman, 9 Vanity Close, Oulton, Stone, Staffs ST15 8TZ.

54 Jack it up

Having lost the use of an arm, I found it difficult to mount timber between centres. I have overcome this with a method which may be of use to other turners with a handicap.

I use a scissor jack with a 150mm 6" length of 38mm 1 1/2" angle iron welded to the top at right angles to the thread at the centre.

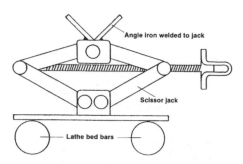

I then simply mark the centres on the workpiece (round or square stock), lay the wood in the angle iron and raise the work by turning the jack screw. It can also be swivelled on the bed bars if necessary.

The work is held on the drive centre as the tailstock is positioned and set, then the jack can be removed. The jack screw thread needs to be kept well greased to allow it to be turned by hand.

Malcolm Maybee, 2 Gordleton Farm Cottages, Silver Street, Sway, Lymington, Hampshire SO41 6DJ.

55 Know your square drill

It is often difficult to drill accurately on the lathe into the end of small square wooden pieces such as pen blanks. I have overcome this difficulty with a safe and simple jig which can be made from a few pieces of scrap timber.

The jig consists of three pieces of wood glued and screwed together. The bottom piece should be of a suitable size to fit snugly between the bed bars of your lathe. The second piece fits over the bed bars, and the third piece should be made of a suitable height so the centre of the workpiece will align with the centre height of the lathe.

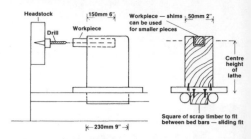

The top piece of wood has a blind slot in it equal in size to the square of the workpiece. The slot can be chiselled out or cut with a router. If you want to drill smaller pieces than the slot size, simply pack either side with shims.

With the workpiece secured in the slot the jig is simply pushed along the bed bars on to the revolving drill in the headstock. Rounding off the back of the jig will make it a more comfortable fit in your hand.

Nick Chapman, 5 Mansfield Drive, Coolcots, Wexford, Ireland.

Although Nick Chapman uses a lathe with round bed bars this method should work equally well with other and older models fitted with other kinds of beds. - Ed.

56 Lathe faceplates from pulleys

Extra lathe faceplates come in handy for permanent mounting of chucks and fixtures. Also, you can leave one faceplate attached to a workpiece for applying a finish while mounting another one for a new turning.

If your headstock has a plain (unthreaded) spindle, you can save considerably by using

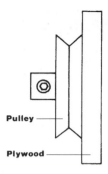

Pulley

Plywood

ordinary pulleys as faceplates. They are inexpensive, come in a wide variety of diameters and bores, and are readily available from your local electric motor shop, hardware store, or DIY store.

I prepare the faceplates by drilling four or five holes through the pulleys and mounting them to a 20mm 3/4" plywood or hardwood disc with screws, then true up the disc on the lathe.

Anthony P. Matlosz, 8 Arlington Drive, Howell, NJ 07731, USA.

57 Light cord pulls

I have produced a number of light cord pulls which throw up a number of niggling problems, the two main ones being wastage and drill wander. I have the ideal solution.

First saw the timber to length. I use 19mm or 25mm 3/4" or 1" square section, cut to the length of the finished pull, but 6mm 1/4" over length. I usually cut 20 or so lengths at a time.

Then, using a pillar drill with a 6mm 1/4" bit, I bore a hole in one end of each piece. This hole is as near centre as possible to a depth about 25mm 1" from the other end.

These lengths are then mounted on the lathe using a steel rod, which is slightly over 6mm diameter, so giving a friction drive just by pushing the workpiece on to the rod. The rod is gripped in a drill chuck mounted on my Masterchuck body. This gives a very positive fixing, rather than a drill chuck with morse taper.

Once mounted I can drill the other end with a 3mm 1/8" drill in the tailstock. As you need only to drill a hole 25mm 1" deep there is no tendency for the drill to wander.

An old fixed centre is then used to support at the tailstock end, and cutting can proceed, including roughing and finishing with the same mounting. The beauty of this method is that both ends of the pull can be fashioned with a skew chisel giving a very good finish, as you can actually cut on to the drive rod and old centre.

There is little wastage, no drill wander and speedy workpiece changeover. Once the pieces have been cut to length and pre-drilled at the bench I can turn 12 finished, polished pulls in 45 minutes.

Neil F. Poston, 46 Littell Tweed, Chelmsford, Essex CM2 6SH.

58 Long small tapers

Here is something I have found in turning long small tapers on wood lathes. I made pool sticks this way. Hold a fingernail-shaped gouge so that it cuts above centre at a long hand-down angle.

You don't need a centre steady. I have shown this idea to a lot of turners, most of them agree.

Try it!

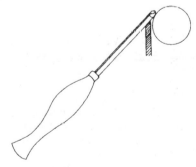

Lloyd P. Humiston, 25800 Corson, Sun City, CA 92355, USA.

59 Long toolrest

When you are turning a long piece between centres the usual toolrest has to be moved several times and this upsets your rhythm, particularly if the shape requires long sweeping cuts. It would be better to have a tool rest for the full length, even if you revert to the short rest for final detail work.

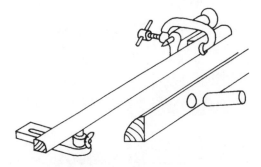

My long tool rest is made of beech. Its left hand end is supported by a rod that fits in the normal base. My rod is steel held in a hole in the wood with epoxy glue (Araldite). For occasional use you might find dowel rod strong enough. At the other end the long rest is held to the tailstock with a cramp, using wood packing to keep it the right distance from the work.

Percy Blandford, Quinton House, Newbold-on-Stour, Stratford-upon-Avon, Warwickshire CV37 8UA.

60 Making a bowl steady

While turning bowls and goblets and the like, I sometimes found it difficult to get the walls as thin as I needed. Proprietary brands of steadies are a bit beyond my pensioner's pocket so I made my own.

Requirements:

An old bicycle hub complete with spindle and nuts.

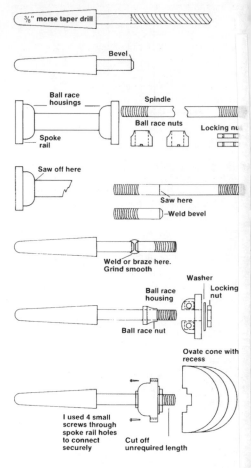

An old morse tapered drill, 10mm 3/8 of an inc will do.

Hacksaw, welding or brazing equipment.

Ruler, scribe, and an engineer's set square.

One pre-turned ovate shaped cone with reces on flat surface.

Step 1 Using the hacksaw, cut the drill flutes from the morse taper shank, as in diagram below.

Step 2 Grind or file a bevel on the remaining stub to facilitate a good weld, as in diagram below.

Step 3 Dismantle the wheel hub. This should leave the spindle housing complete with race

arings, the spindle, two race bearing nuts and
lo locking nuts, as in diagram.

ep 4 Take the spindle housing and saw off
e end, as shown.

ep 5 Take the spindle and saw off from one
nd roughly 12mm 1/2" from the end of the
read. Then bevel the cut end of the short stub
s was done to the morse taper stub, see
agram.

ep 6 Line up both stubs and weld or braze
gether. Care must be taken at this point
ecause the morse taper's shape can make the
ing up difficult. See diagram.

ep 7 Thread on specially-shaped ball race nut
own to the lowest thread. Then push on
parated ball race housing, followed by a flat
asher and a locking nut. See diagram. Do not
er-tighten as ball race and housing should be
le to rotate freely.

ep 8 The last job is to mount the pre-turned
ate cone, and screw secure. If the thread
ngth left after the locking nut has been
sitioned is too long do as I did - cut it off. See
agram.

hen the bowl steady is mounted in the tail stock
d pushed up tight to the completed inner bowl,
cellent steadiness can be almost guaranteed. I
ve made several different sized ovate cones
d also flat plates for the very large bowls.
crap wood for this I have in plenty; good wood
r the bowls etc. is expensive.

. Goodman, 24 Waterloo Road, Newport,
went NP9 4FP.

. Goodman, 24 Waterloo Road, Newport,
went NP9 4FP.

61 Mandrel for wheel-making

Here is an idea for turning a set of identical
wheels quickly.

Insert a 6mm 1/4" T Nut in the centre of a
wooden faceplate. Screw a length of 6mm 1/4"
studding or Allthread into the T Nut and tighten it
well.

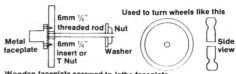

Precut wheel discs are drilled centrally and
placed together on the threaded rod. Secure
them with a washer and nut. Turning can now
begin, thus ensuring a set of wheels all of the
same diameter.

*Lloyd P. Humiston, 25800 Corson Avenue,
Sun City, CA 92584, USA.*

62 Marking burrs for bowls

We were interested in Dave Regester's wheeze
for marking out a burr with end-grain sealer to
assess where to cut for turning a bowl.
(*Woodturning* issue 9, pages 37- 8).

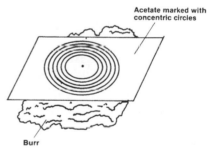

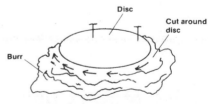

We suggest two quick and accurate methods
which have the added advantage of being usable
either way up (for rough top or bottom styles) and
for choosing appropriate points of balance in both
the literal and design sense.

The first method is to use an acetate (overhead projector transparency) or piece of clear plastic like Perspex with concentric circles marked on it at 25mm 1" intervals. Move this over the piece holding the burr underneath to easily locate the centre most appropriate for balance.

The second method is to use thin ply or cardboard discs cut to the appropriate size and attach to the burr with a couple of panel pins. No marking is required, just cut.

We use both methods routinely for natural edge and burr pieces in our workshop.

Bob and Ann Phillips, RD1 Upper Moutere, Nelson, New Zealand.

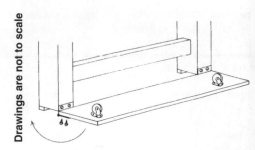

Drawings are not to scale

63 Measuring idea

When turning and I need to measure accurately a width, depth or thickness of 12mm 1/2" or less, I use the shank of a twist drill of the appropriate size as a measuring gauge to set my callipers. This method is also useful when setting the depth gauge on a router.

You can also put two drill bits side by side, e.g. 12mm 1/2" and 10mm 3/8" to get 22mm 7/8". However, you cannot do this with three bits unless you set up a jig to ensure their centres are in line.

Another tip: when turning or working cork or rubber, freeze it first. The material will not then flex when a tool is applied.

J.G. Holyoak, Mead Cottage, 69 New Road, Blakeney, Holt, Norfolk NR25 7PA.

64 Mobile bench and lathe

Being blessed with a small workshop and cursed with a bad back, I have devised this method for shifting my bench/lathe etc. out of the way when not in use.

I use a stout pair of castors fitted to a piece of 20mm 3/4" ply. A pair of strong flap hinges are fitted under the ply and on to the bottom of my bench legs.

A small block, fitted on the other side of the legs, compensates for the hinge protuberance.

I have fitted this arrangement to both ends of my bench-lathe and band saw stand.

All I do is lift up one end and then the other, kick the castor board under, and - hey presto! - the lot is mobile, no more dragging about. In the case of a metal base, I drill and bolt the hinge on and, when the bench is in use, I carry out the procedure in reverse and all is then solid.

My bench, by the way, is a rather hefty 1980mm 6'6" long by 915mm 3' wide by 840mm 2'9" deep. My wooden lathe stand is 1525mm 5' long by 840mm 2'9" high. The bed is 305mm 12" wide by 100mm 4" deep and the legs 100mm 4" by 75mm 3".

G.F. Short, 32 Firs Road, Caldicot, Newport, Gwent NP6 4DQ.

65 Mobile tool stands

Mobile stands for grinder and chisels could be the answer for woodturners who have to operate in confined spaces.

I recycled two old computer monitor arms, the type that fix to desktops and allow the screen to be adjusted to different heights and positions on a swinging arm. Second-hand office equipment suppliers are a good source.

The mobile stands enable chisels and the grinder to be easily swung into position

The grinder is mounted on one with a single arm, allowing the grinder to be positioned at nearly chest height.

If a spring-loaded unit is used, as I have done, then a locking screw will need to be drilled and tapped to lock the height but still allow the unit to swing. This enables it to be put away when not in use.

The height of the tool holder can be much lower than the grinder, and less weight, therefore a double arm unit can be used. This can be used much closer to the working position.

In both cases the stand on the top of the arm, for the computer monitor, has been removed and a board suitably drilled attached.

It is here I have solved another problem; where to keep the sandpapers being used? Onto the board with the chisels I have formed a container to hold my assortment of partly-used sandpapers.

Both arms are attached to the metal end leg of the lathe stand by drilling and tapping the

mounting unit. If readers have a bench-mounted lathe the arms can be mounted in the same way as they would on a desk.

Bryan Hawkins, 54 Woodman Drive, Tawa, Wellington 6006, New Zealand.

66 Modification to older Jubilee lathe

I want to extend the capacity at the outboard end of my Union Jubilee lathe, particularly to accommodate an Axminster four-jaw chuck. I came up with this cheap and simple modification.

This method means the toolrest has to be rigged from the spindle end of the lathe but this takes no more than five.minutes.

This washer would probably benefit from being manufactured with a spigot to take up clearance between spindle and table, as indicated.

All material mild steel.

50mm 2" DIA
25mm 1"
1" DIA
25mm 1"
Threaded to suit Jubilee toolpost screw
63mm 2½"

63mm 2½" DIA
12mm ½" UNC nut
35mm 1⅜"
6mm ¼"
Threaded UNC 12mm ½"
100mm 4"
100mm 4"
180mm 7"
45mm 1¾"
12mm ½" DIA
22mm ⅞" DIA
32mm 1¼" DIA
25mm 1" DIA

The method entails making use of the original toolrest with an additional sleeve to increase the working height and substituting a new, larger threaded spindle for the locking mechanism.

The drawings clearly show what is required and if you do not have access to a metalworking lathe or a model engineer friend, then any light

37

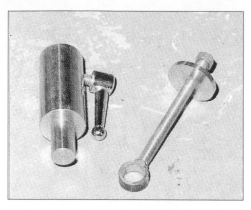

engineering firm will produce the two components.

When you wish to revert to spindle-turning the original rest components are used.

I have used this facility considerably since manufacture and found it to be totally functional in all respects.

Keith Brown, 2 Victory Road, Stubbington, Fareham, Hants PO14 2SA.

67 Modified compression/ expansion chuck

I much enjoyed reading the article 'A Modified Compression Expansion Chuck' in Issue 5 of *Woodturning*. I had already made a similar chuck, but with further modifications to give more universal use.

I started with a three-jaw scroll chuck fitted with a set of three blank soft jaws. I got a steel disc 125mm 5" DIA x 6mm 1/4" thick and drilled a centre hole 12mm 1/2" DIA. This was to take a bolt which could be screwed into a nut held in the chuck, pulling the disc on to the jaws. After checking that the disc was properly centred, I welded the back of the disc to the jaws.

I then cut the disc into three parts which allowed me to use it for mounting the wooden jaws as mentioned in the article.

The faceplate can also be used as an expansion

Chuck and disc with the jaws closed

Chuck and disc with the jaws partly open

The chuck fitted with a wooden drum. This is used as a sander by fitting abrasive paper round the circumference and also flat on the face

faceplate. The disc has then to be ground slightly conical round its circumference.

A further adaptation was to put screws in the holes used for mounting the wooden jaws. These screws could be used as three jaws for holding blanks which are too small to go on the wooden faceplate.

The metal disc gives enough support to keep the wooden jaws aligned and so you do not need stabilising bars or alignment plates on the back.

Frank Valgaeren, 36 Benoitlaan, 2550 Kontich, Belgium.

68 Multi-jaws for Multistar

Owners of Multistar chucks may be interested in the following idea.

Home-made wooden jaws can be made from smaller diameter stock than the 60mm 2 3/8" recommended in the chuck manual. This is done by using the collar jaws (split rings) as shown in the sketch.

After turning, the jaws are cut into four segments, each segment is numbered in sequence, returned to the chuck, and bored to the size required.

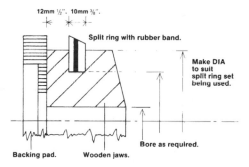

12mm ½". 10mm ⅜".

Split ring with rubber band.

Make DIA to suit split ring set being used.

Bore as required.

Backing pad.   Wooden jaws.

This is ideal for turning small objects from oddments found in the scrap box.

My first set were made from the stump of the stock left after turning a small lidded box from oak held by the split rings.

B.R. Stephens, 69 Richmond Hill, Oldbury, Warley, West Midlands B68 9TH.

69 No more wayward ways

For those woodturners who do not possess a drill press of sufficient throat to accurately produce a hole for the insertion of say a screw chuck, I suggest the following idea. Obtain a square blank of wood with a flat bottom, say 12mm 1/2" thick and make a drill bush to suit the diameter of the drill to be used.

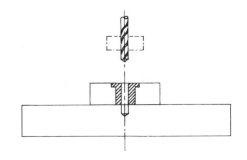

Drill a hole to suit the drill bush location diameter and press it into the wood base. Mark a centre on the blank, locate the drill in the bush, place it on the previously marked centre and proceed to drill to the required depth with the wooden block held squarely in contact with the blank. This will produce the required hole in any position on any size blank at right angles to the surface. The depth of hole can be regulated by the use of any proprietary collar, to suit the drill, locked in position.

Bill Newton, 5 Beacon Brow, Horton Bank Top, Bradford, Yorkshire BD6 3DE.

70 Non-slip floor

Having recently enlarged my workshop to accommodate two students as well as myself, I found the new floor rather too slippery for safety. I found the ideal solution was to lay the new No-Rip roofing felt from Rubberoid. The top, sanded surface is non-slip yet easy to keep clean.

The material comes on a standard size roll, about a metre wide, and is nailed down with clout nails. It could be fixed with adhesive to a solid floor. Lay it on a warm day as it will be easier to cut, and when it cools it shrinks to a tight fit without any bubbles or wrinkles.

It does get tacky at very high temperatures - approaching 100° F, and the other drawback is that it is more expensive than ordinary felt, but I think the extra expense is worth it.

E.D. Farrow, 76 Langford Cottages, Lavant, Chichester, West Sussex PO18 0JR.

71 Parting saw versus parting chisel

Tools are too expensive today to be wasted. So that when a bandsaw breaks at the weld before it has served a normal working life and it is not too blunt to cut, I feel something must be done so that its still usable remainder can be put to some purpose. So...

Break off say 230mm 9" or 255mm 10" of the saw and screw it into your padsaw handle. Pencil mark the circumference line of 'cut-off' and, with your diamond-ended parting chisel, scribe this line 3mm 1/8" to 6mm 1/4" deep with the chisel on its FLAT on the tool rest.

Now, departing from the customary principle of sawing of a still workpiece and a moving blade, adjust your lathe revs to about half the normal and switch on. You work from the under side of course and have mounted the blade in the padsaw handle to cut on the 'draw'.

Only gentle pressure should be applied at first but, when the blade has cut itself into its full width, the blade can be slowly drawn back and forth and the lathe's revs brought back to normal.

My lathe is a 20-year old Coronet Junior and has only two speeds but I find it quite safe and simple, once you have found the right gauge of blade and speed of lathe. I find it best to stop spinning about 12mm 1/2" before severance and finish off manually, or the workpiece can become air-borne! A moment on the sandwheel and the job contrasts quite well with a chisel job and is quicker too. Indeed, I resort to it quite frequently. It's novel, unwasteful, it's a way out and it's fun!

Some, however, may regard it as a crazy daft idea of a silly old 85-year-old!

H.A. Sawyer, 'Thatches', Staplehay, Taunton TA3 7HB.

72 Parting tool (1)

I have made a simple but effective parting tool from a used HSS engineering power saw blade.

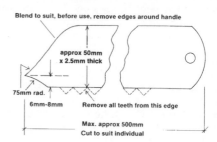

This could be obtained from an engineering company or a steel stockist. It does not require a handle but it would be safer to have one, even a laminated one. Once made the 'regrind life' is fantastic.

R.G. Long, Brooklea, Ford, Chippenham, Wilts SN14 8RR.

73 Parting tool (2)

I have often heard of turners using old power hacksaw blades to make parting tools (see Tip 72) - I have made and used one myself.

I would also like to suggest using an old forged steel knife blade with integral bolster and tang, as found in bone-handled knives.

If the blade is cut off about 50–60mm 2"–2 1/2" out from the bolster it gives a perfectly strong tool with no instability in use, yet will give a 1mm 1/32" cut.

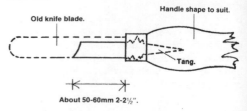

A thin parting tool like this means minimal grain mismatch when making the base and lid of a box. Use a scrap piece of wood glued inside the lid to form a spigot to fit into the base.

A forged blade like this is stronger than a mechanical hacksaw blade, which is designed to be used in tension, and provided care is taken in grinding, the steel is ideal.

The blade in section is triangular, which makes for a good parting tool. I use it upside down, the same as a fluted parting tool.

Stan Kenny, 24 Kirkliston Gardens, Belfast, N. Ireland BT5 6EE.

74 Pin chuck alternative

A twin-splined internal chuck which can be used as an alternative to a pin chuck is an idea I have devised.

Provided the vaned or splined driving centre (chuck) is tapped well into the 12mm 1/2" pre-drilled hole in the workpiece and the solid or revolving centre is brought up to the opposite end, any rough, out of balance timber can be turned safely.

I experienced no vibrations or movement in or from the workpiece.

The device would be best used in a three-to-four jaw chuck. The shaft can be made from steel bar from 8mm 5/16" round up to 25mm 1".

The materials I have used are a 12mm 1/2" round steel rod, 1–2mm 3/64–3/32" hard flat steel, 15–20mm 5/8–3/4" wide and 25–35mm 1"–1 3/8" deep.

The method I used was to hacksaw the round bar down the centre to a depth of 60mm 2 3/8". Weld up the slot on both sides, leaving 20mm 3/4" in the centre open.

Dress off the surplus weld, making the bar circular again. Carefully drive the flat steel

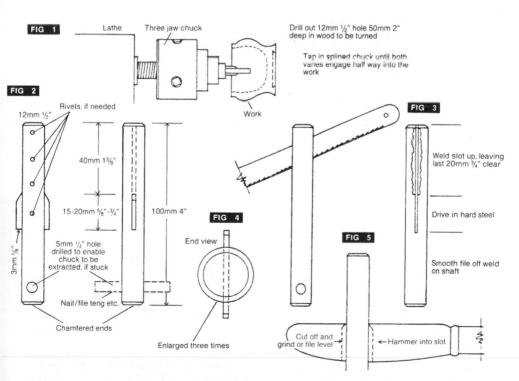

FIG 1 — Lathe — Three jaw chuck — Drill out 12mm ½" hole 50mm 2" deep in wood to be turned. Tap in splined chuck until both vanes engage half way into the work. Work

FIG 2 — Rivets, if needed — 12mm ½" — 40mm 1⅝" — 15-20mm ⅝"-¾" — 100mm 4" — 5mm ¼" hole drilled to enable chuck to be extracted, if stuck — Nail/file teng etc. — Chamfered ends — 3mm ⅛"

FIG 3 — Weld slot up, leaving last 20mm ¾" clear — Drive in hard steel — Smooth file off weld on shaft

FIG 4 — End view — Enlarged three times

FIG 5 — Cut off and grind or file level — ←Hammer into slot

41

through the slot until equal amounts appear at both sides. This steel should now be held solid in the bar/rod.

If not, a 3mm 1/8" hole should be drilled through the centre and a rivet hammered home.

Cut off the file down the protruding flat steel to the shape shown in the diagram, leaving about 3mm 1/8" either side. Chamfer the ends of the bar.

If you don't have welding facilities, rivet the length of the slot together, remembering to allow for the sawn-out steel by packing or shimming out to the original dimensions of rod/bar.

A 5mm 3/16" hole bored through the end nearest the headstock helps when removing the chuck from the turned workpiece.

John Walton, Riseholme, 25 Hill Terrace, Middleton-in-Teesdale, County Durham DL12 0SL.

75 Pocket centre finder

The usual centre square, whether a separate tool or part of a combination square, has a blade longer than we need for most purposes and that can be a nuisance on small work.

A centre finder for use on rounds or squares up to 50mm 2" is easy and accurate to use, while being compact enough to carry in a pocket.

The principle is the same - you put the tool against the circumference of a round object or the corner of a square and draw a line, then move to another position and draw again, so the lines cross at the centre.

The two parts could be 6mm 1/4" hardwood. Cut the top piece with a straight edge along a diameter to within 20mm 3/4" of the opposite side. Make the bottom piece with a 90° cutout from a matching point.

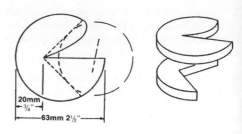

Glue the two pieces together so the straight edge bisects the right angle. The outline does not have to be a circle, but as a turner you may wish to mount the gadget in the lathe and true its outline.

Percy Blandford, Quinton House, Newbold-on-Stour, Stratford-upon-Avon, Warwickshire CV37 8UA.

76 Preparing end of spindles

My lathe is an older US Sears & Roebuck, 16 speed, 1/3 Horse Power, Single Tube Lathe. I have a copy crafter, a four jaw-chuck, plus all the accessories offered by Sears & Roebuck. The lathe has been modified to reverse (for light sanding and finishing) and I have filled the main tube bed with concrete for damping of vibrations and stiffness.

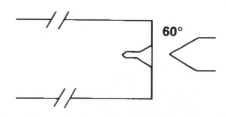

I use a machinist's centre drill to prepare end of spindles to fit the tail stock. This drill makes a hole like the one shown in the diagram in one operation.

The tip of the tailstock centres thus, enters the small hole and only the sides of cone bear on the wood.

I have never read anything on using this drill in any woodworking publications. It works for me!

The method keeps the split out of very small spindles down. I made a great number of spindles with 10mm 3/8" tenons for baby cradle sides.

Paul H. Jaenichen, 24 Lakeshore Parkway, Brandenburg, KY 40108-9325, USA.

77 Protection from jaws

With a four-jaw chuck there is always the danger that the revolving sharp edges of the protruding jaws can catch your fingers or clothing.

With this in mind, when I recently bought a four jaw chuck I thought it a good idea to wrap a piece of motor cycle tyre inner tube round the outside of the chuck and jaws.

This not only smooths the sharp edges but it also stops the jaws from falling out of the chuck body if you open them out too far - see photo.

Michael Pavey, 1 North Close, Draycott, Cheddar, Somerset BS27 3TY.

78 Rawlbolt chuck

I found when using the pin chuck on my combination chuck system that if the hole was not exact, the work could become loose. I have overcome this by using a Rawlbolt which expands as you tighten it.

I bought some odd Rawlbolts for 30p each at a car boot sale. They were 10mm 3/8" DIA but designed to fit into a 15mm 5/8" hole. I removed the bolt and got another bolt of the same thread but threaded all the way up to the head.

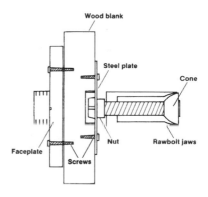

Next I trued up a wood blank and cut a recess in the centre to take the head of the bolt. The bolt head is held in place with a steel plate screwed to the wood, centre drilled with a 10mm hole. A nut is screwed on to the bolt tight up to the steel plate, which holds it very firmly (see diagram).

The Rawlbolt is then reassembled using a rubber ring to hold the jaws together - I used a finger off an old rubber glove. The workpiece is put on the bolt and tightened up until the expanding jaws grip firmly.

I have found this a cheap and efficient way of improving a pin chuck.

Robert Peterson, Westview Cottage, West End, Stainforth, Doncaster, South Yorkshire DN7 5SA.

Rear toolrest support

Free-standing rear tool supports are becoming increasingly popular, but they can be expensive to buy. I use a Myford ML8 lathe mounted on a metal cabinet. To enable better use of the standard rear tool post I have made my own tripod support which is simple in use and very robust.

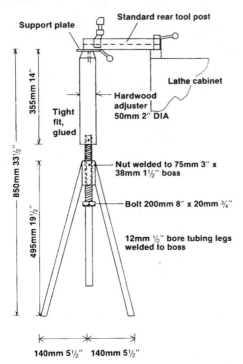

Support plate

Standard rear tool post

355mm 14"

850mm 33¹/₂"

495mm 19¹/₂"

Tight fit, glued

Lathe cabinet

Hardwood adjuster 50mm 2" DIA

Nut welded to 75mm 3" x 38mm 1¹/₂" boss

Bolt 200mm 8" x 20mm ³/₄"

12mm ¹/₂" bore tubing legs welded to boss

140mm 5¹/₂"   140mm 5¹/₂"

It consists of a 355mm 14" x 50mm 2" DIA length of hardwood, three lengths of 12mm 1/2" bore tubing welded into a tripod, and a 200mm 8" x 20mm 3/4" threaded bolt running through a nut welded into a central boss of 75mm 3" x 38mm 1 1/2" DIA. On top of the hardwood adjuster is a support plate 75mm x 25mm x 6mm 3" x 1" x 1/4" of plastic or acetal, screwed on with a single countersunk woodscrew so that it is free to revolve.

Having positioned and locked the rear tool post ready for turning it is a simple matter to place the tripod so it supports the tool rest, using the screw adjustment to make a firm contact.

Using a bit of imagination in the source and choice of materials the support can be made at minimal cost. My support has an operating height of 850mm 33 1/2", but dimensions can of course be adjusted to suit most lathes with an integral tool post.

Reg Long, Brooklea, Ford, Chippenham, Wilts SN14 8RR.

Rechucking

It was with interest that I read Dave Regester's article on page 55 of issue 2, particularly his rechucking method as I feel that the system I have devised for myself is a lot simpler and just as effective.

Since I work relatively green wood, rough turning, followed by rechucking later, is necessary. I turn the outside shape first, cutting a dovetail to receive my expanding collets on my Axminster 4 jaw self-centring chuck. I then remount blank for roughing out and cut a further dovetail on the base of the bowl, leaving sufficient wall thickness for truing up later.

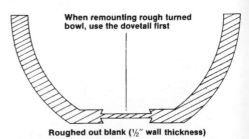

When remounting rough turned bowl, use the dovetail first

Roughed out blank (¹/₂" wall thickness)

I remount the roughed out bowl several weeks later when fully dried out, using the dovetail and cut on the inside base. I simply finish the outside of the bowl, remove and remount on the outer dovetail and finish the inside, turning off the inner dovetail. (See sketch).

A modified chuck key may be necessary to get into those awkward places, but a machined Allen key is a cheap alternative.

Obviously the two possible problems are 1: Depth of bowl that can be roughed out - in my case with my Coronet No 3 the maximum overhang on the headstock is 5" though depths of 7" can be achieved with specially adapted wooden jaws and 2: Safety - positive rechucking is essential.

Before I bought my Axminster chuck a year ago I used the Craft Supplies chuck in a similar fashion but doubted the safety of the operation. As the dovetailed recess became oval during the drying process, I was wary of how well the roughed out bowl was re-secured - a problem not as evident on the Axminster chuck as you can apply more pressure when locking out.

Claran McCarthy, Cloydagh, Carlow, Rep. of Ireland.

Recycled brace and bits

I had a number of short spoon bits with square shanks for use in a conventional carpenter's brace, I wanted to use these bits as turning gouges, but I didn't want to laboriously grind all the square shanks to form tangs for individual handles.

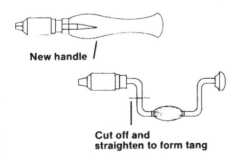

New handle

Cut off and straighten to form tang

Instead, I cut the chuck off an old brace, formed a tang and fitted this into a new turned handle. Now I can use all the spoon bits in just one handle.

William Hopcyn Jones, 37 Station Road, Llangennech, Llanelli, Dyfed SA14 8UD.

Roller blind

I have come up with a method for keeping woodturners' workshops user-friendly.

Simply get a 1525mm 5ft wide roller blind and fix it to the ceiling of the shop. Then pull the blind down whenever you are roughing down or whatever you are turning.

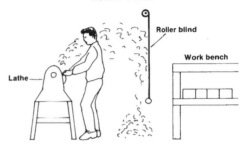

Roller Blind

The chippings and shavings go over your shoulders, hit the blind and drop to the floor in a straight line for easy sweeping up.

I am sure this tip will prove very useful to people with small workshops and who have lots of tools hanging around and do not want to have to move them all when tidying up.

D. Hall, 21 Deacon Way, Banbury, Oxon OX16 0DY.

83 Rotating chisel holder

When turning it is useful to have several chisels handy without leaving them scattered over the workbench to get covered in shavings. My revolving chisel-holder keeps them handy and tidy at the same time.

The holder is based on a 255mm 10" DIA disc of 10mm 3/8" ply or other suitable material, suspended on a 10mm 3/8" DIA dowel rod. There

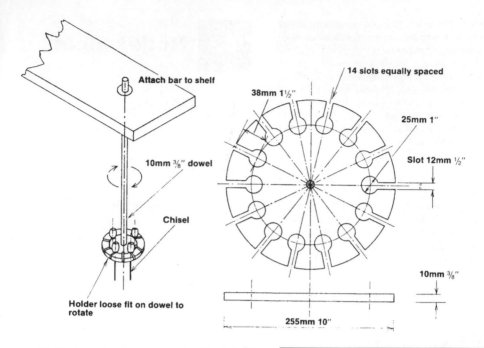

Attach bar to shelf

10mm ⅜" dowel

Chisel

Holder loose fit on dowel to rotate

14 slots equally spaced

38mm 1½"

25mm 1"

Slot 12mm ½"

10mm ⅜"

255mm 10"

are 14 slots equally spaced round the disc to hold the chisels. The size of the slots can of course be adjusted to suit your chisels.

I have my holder fitted under a shelf above my lathe, but it could be fitted to the ceiling if more convenient.

S.D. Wildin, 14 Summerleaze, Lydney, Gloucester GL15 5PS.

84 | Sanding drum

I have used the following methods of making a sanding drum or sanding stick for some time and hope they will be of use to others.

The first method is to use the chuck body on a drill. A strip of garnet paper or emery paper (the roll type is preferable as it is much stronger than sheet) is cut long enough to go around the chuck body 2–3 times at least. A piece of Blu-Tack or Pritt Stick etc. is used sparingly to stick one end of the paper to the chuck body. The paper is then

wrapped around the chuck body and the end piece stuck down using the same principle as before. Only a small amount is needed so as not to cause a bump in the paper. It is important to wrap the paper around the chuck so that rotation causes the paper to tighten on the chuck body. With this method the cloth can be removed for normal use of the chuck.

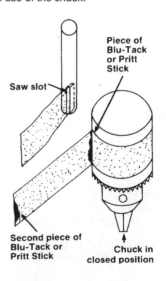

Piece of Blu-Tack or Pritt Stick

Saw slot

Second piece of Blu-Tack or Pritt Stick

Chuck in closed position

46

The second method is to use a piece of dowel or metal bar. Cut a saw slot in one end. This must be as deep as the paper or cloth is wide. The bar or dowel is then put into the chuck and turned around the spindle a few times before the end is stuck down. As the paper becomes dull it can be cut back and stuck down again ready to re-use.

These methods can be used for radiusing, buffing, polishing and sanding metal or wood. They can also be used on a pedestal drill or pistol drill.

R.J. Ball, 65 Keyham Lane, Humberstone, Leicester LE5 1FH.

 85 | # Safe faceplate fixing

I have devised this method for really safe and secure faceplate fixing of large pieces of timber by inserting four trunnions or barrel nuts into the blank. If the lathe is securely bolted down, it is possible even to oit on a 610mm 24" long log when it is attached to the faceplate in this way.

First turn the log between centres to true the ends and trim the sides. This makes it easier to mark and drill the necessary holes later.

Then drill four 10mm 3/8" clearance holes in a suitably-sized faceplate (FIG 1) and mark through these holes on to the end of the log or blank to be turned. Drill 10mm 3/8" clearance holes about 63mm 2 1/2" deep into the log end. Draw diagonal lines through the holes on the log end and continue the lines down the side of the log.

The four trunnions or barrel nuts, each about 25mm 1" long x 15mm 5/8" or 20mm 3/4" DIA (FIG 2) are inserted into holes drilled into the side of the log about 50mm 2" from the end. The holes are drilled on the previously drawn lines so they meet the holes drilled in the end.

The trunnions have tapped 3/8" holes drilled through them to take 3/8" threaded studding which passes through the faceplate and down the holes drilled in the log end (FIG 3). The studding is secured to the faceplate with nuts and washers.

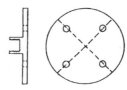

FIG 1 Faceplate drilled with four 10mm 3/8" clearance holes.

Tapped 3/8" hole

FIG 2   Trunnions 25mm 1" long x 15mm 5/8" or 20mm 3/4" DIA.

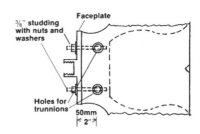

3/8" studding with nuts and washers

Faceplate

Holes for trunnions 50mm |← 2"→|

FIG 3   Log fixed to faceplate.

After hollowing out and shaping the vessel it is reversed and the bottom turned in the usual way to remove the holes.

Gordon Clarke, The Spinning Gallery, Market Place, Marazion, Penzance, Cornwall TR11 0AR.

86 | # Save polish– and mess

A good idea, which can save polish, lacquer and mess, is to wrap soft beeswax polish in a piece of cloth and secure with an elastic band, rather like a French polish rubber. Polish oozes through the cloth and is not splattered around.

Lacquer (melamine) I decant into a small mustard jar, drilling two holes in the plastic top to control flow when needed. Grease the thread of the plastic top for easy removal.

These two methods of application help keep my helmet visor clear of sprayed particles.

P.G. Gutteridge, Four Winds, Glengolly, Thurso, Caithness KW14 7XP.

87 Short turnings

It can be difficult to turn short pieces of wood between centres because of holding problems, and the difficulty of positioning even the shortest toolrest close enough to be effective.

I found this solution when I wanted to turn a piece of rosewood 38mm 1 1/2" long x 20mm 3/4" square to a cylinder.

I mounted an Axminster four-jaw chuck on the headstock spindle and gripped a Tyme two-prong mini drive centre in the chuck which gave me a clear projection of 85mm 3 1/4" at the headstock end.

After marking the centres on each end of the workpiece I wound up the tailstock with live centre to grip it firmly enough to turn. The extension thus gained enabled me to use a 200mm 8" toolrest comfortably and safely.

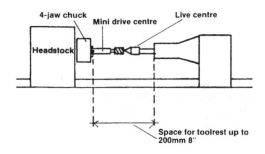

With a custom-made 90mm 3 1/2" toolrest I could probably work down to the smallest length and diameter needed by anyone. No doubt this idea could be adapted to other chucking systems.

Colin Greenaway, 162 Stourvale Road, Southbourne, Bournemouth BH6 5HJ.

88 Simple bowl steady and live centre

I read with interest G. Goodman's Top Tip for a bowl steady in issue no. 7 (Tip 59). However, as I have little or no facilities for metal working or welding I would like to explain my simpler system I devised some months ago.

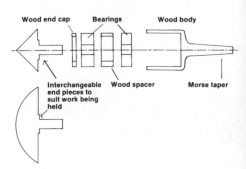

I cannot give any dimensions as the size of the whole device depends on the size of bearings available and the size of morse taper.

As I have the tendencies of a magpie I came across a pair of hoarded ball-races 25mm 1" DIA with a 6mm 1/4" bore with which to make a live centre.

For the body I turned a piece of beech of appropriate length to a morse taper on one end and then used this morse taper in the headstock to bore a true hole for the bearings and sleeves. The bearings should be a tight fit so as not to rotate. The two wooden sleeves should be glued in to make sure the bearings do not move.

The rotating end can of course be made to suit any shape that requires support and when fitted with a spindle that is just tight enough to grip the centre of the bearings you have a live tail centre with interchangeable ends - all for the price of two bearings and an hour's work.

If you have to buy the bearings look under Bearing Stockists in the Yellow Pages. I have found the wooden parts strong enough for most applications. If parts do wear out they can always be replaced cheaply and easily.

W.D. Colgrave, 3 Hanover Drive, Winsford, Cheshire CW7 1PP.

89 Soft touch

When turning rounded objects, such as eggs, between centres, you are often left with small rough areas at the ends which need final smoothing.

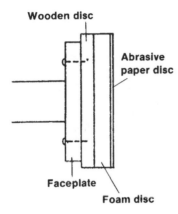

Wooden disc

Abrasive paper disc

Faceplate

Foam disc

I have made my own padded sanding disc which is ideal. It is simply a fine-grade abrasive paper disc glued to a disc of industrial-quality foam about 25mm 1" thick. This in turn is glued to a wooden disc which is screwed to the lathe faceplate.

The cushioned effect of the disc gives an ideal fine finish.

Jon Morton, 70 Corisande Road, Selly Oak, Birmingham B29 6RP.

90 Sore patches salved

Rough grain or 'sore' patches on the outside of bowls is something we all encounter at some time. A lot is written and talked about reversing a lathe's rotation to solve this problem, but if, like me, you don't have a reversing switch, try this method.

Mount the blank on a faceplate or screwchuck and turn the outside to shape with a spigot, foot, recess, or whatever, to suit the chucking method used to turn the inside at a later stage. If the foot is to remain on the bowl, finish, sand and polish.

Sand the rest of the outside of the bowl with power discs or by hand, to around 120–150 grit, but not too fine.

Remove the bowl and remount it on the chuck for turning the inside. The bowl is now spinning in the opposite direction (i.e.'reversed'). Now sand the outside to a finish, removing the rough patches before turning the inside.

Gavin Chapman, 21 Caernarvon Avenue, Garforth, Leeds LS25 2LQ.

91 Space-saver stand

Space can be saved in a small workshop by mounting your bandsaw on a rotating table. My bandsaw is rectangular, 760mm 30" x 485mm 19".

Having plenty of wood I opted to build my own bench stand for the saw, topping it off with an offcut of 30mm 1 1/8" thick kitchen worktop.

The bandsaw was then bolted to another piece of 30mm 1 1/8" worktop and an ideal axis arrived at, with cardboard templates, so the saw could be parked in its best position with least intrusion into the working area.

When I was satisfied with the axis, I drilled a 10mm 3/8" hole through both pieces of worktop, and inserted a length of 8mm 5/16" threaded rod through the holes. Washers and locking nuts were then fitted to provide a secure, yet loose, fit between the two layers of worktop.

When not in use, the bandsaw is kept along the back wall of the shed, but when needed it can be easily swivelled through approximately 90°. Obviously care will be needed if your saw is a heavy model.

Originally, I assumed a locking device would be needed for the sawing position, and this was easily done with a peg dropped through a top layer hole into a bottom layer hole, but experience has shown this to be unnecessary.

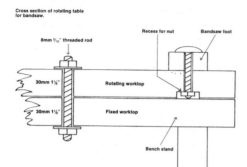

Cross section of rotating table for bandsaw.

Indeed, there is a further benefit in being able to position the bandsaw in any position, because extra-long pieces of wood can be cut with their ends protruding through the open doorway.

Finally, I fitted an old curtain across the bandsaw's parked position to protect it from flying wood chips during turning.

Bob Musgrave, 18 Mildred Road, Walton, Street, Somerset BA16 9QR.

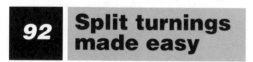

92 Split turnings made easy

To make split turnings the usual method is to glue the two halves of the wood blank together with a piece of paper sandwiched between them so the pieces can be prised apart with a knife after turning.

However, I have had some failures with this method, particularly when one piece is slightly coarser or softer grained than the other. This can result in the centres running over to one side and one half ending up slightly smaller than the other.

My centring system avoids that problem, and you do not need to wait for glue to set.

All you need are two short lengths of square metal tube and two hardwood plugs shouldered to fit tightly into one end of each length of tube. You can use a number of different sized tubes to suit the size of turning.

Cut square spigots on each end of your joined blank as shown and the metal tubes and plugs go on each spigot. The lathe centres fit into the wooden plugs.

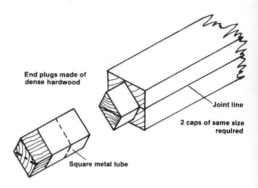

Make sure the tube, plugs and spigots are all dead square and a good tight fit. Make the spigots about 1mm 1/16" longer than the depth of recess in the tube so that the whole arrangement locks up solidly when centred in the lathe.

Careful centring ensures that the device can be used many times with no loss of accuracy, especially if used with a revolving centre.

Ray Willis, 34 Blackmoor Wood, Ascot, Berkshire SL5 8EN.

93 Stop wandering drills

The problem of drill wander while drilling holes for light pulls can be overcome by adopting this method.

Roughly saw scrap into square cross section to the length of the finished light pull.

Using a bench drill press, drill cord holes and

countersink for the cord knot, centring the entry point of the drill by eye.

Mount a scrap of hardwood at the headstock (I use a four-jaw chuck), then turn a taper to give in effect a solid centre.

Mount the blank between the headstock centre and tailstock revolving centre. Turn the blank to shape using friction drive. This is quite satisfactory and means the lathe need never be stopped when mounting blanks or reworking.

P.G. Gutteridge, Four Winds, Glengolly, Thurso, Caithness KW14 7XP.

94 Switchgear solution

There is no need for a separate panic button or foot switch and trailing leads to get in your way if your lathe switch box is fitted to slide along a rail fixed to the front of your lathe bench.

Metal electrical conduit is fine for the job and it should be fixed along the whole length of the bench using wooden blocks at either end just like a towel rail.

Screw the switch box onto a backing board of ply or MDF which has nylon or wooden runners and a spacer fitted to the back, the runners being a good friction fit on the rail.

Run the electrical cables under the bench top and up the back to the lathe motor and the electrical outlet. Keep the cables under light tension to prevent them trailing by fixing them to the back of the bench or to the wall with an elastic band or a spring.

Check for where the cables rub against the bench and wall and sleeve them with plastic hosepipe to prevent the insulation from being damaged. Check the cables periodically for damage.

This system could also be used for the positioning of overhead lighting but a slotted board will give more options for the positioning of a light or lights as well as give you some lathe work turning up the fittings to run in the slots.

R.W. Fernie, Gourdiemuir, Glenfoot, Abernethy, Perthshire PH2 9LS, Scotland.

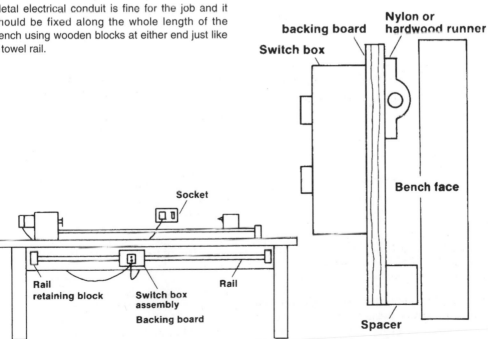

Socket

Rail   **Rail**
retaining block   **Switch box assembly**
Backing board

backing board   **Nylon or hardwood runner**
Switch box
Bench face
Spacer

95 Tailstock centre tray

Users of certain short-bed lathes may have found as I have, that the tailstock centre can be a nuisance when turning on the faceplate or chuck.

The problem takes two forms:

1. Unless the tailstock centre is removed it can be very painful against the elbow.

2. The tailstock saddle, drawn to the extreme end of the bed, cannot easily be secured since the locking handle will not turn past the end bracket. The result is an irritating vibration chatter whilst the lathe is running.

I have solved both problems to my own satisfaction with the gadget described below. It costs, incidentally, almost nothing.

A tray was made with battens fixed to the underside. The tray size I found most useful is about 150mm 6" x 230mm 9". The inside face of the battens was lined with strips of rubber and so set as to make a tight fit over bed bars.

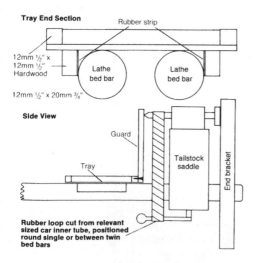

Tray End Section

Rubber strip

12mm ½" x 12mm ½" Hardwood

Lathe bed bar

Lathe bed bar

12mm ½" x 20mm ¾"

Side View

Guard

Tray

Tailstock saddle

End bracket

Rubber loop cut from relevant sized car inner tube, positioned round single or between twin bed bars

A piece of plywood, with the top corners rounded over, was attached to the end of the tray by two screws into the tray edge.

The tray is set onto the bars and against the point of the centre (see diagram).

To prevent the saddle bolt vibrating, a piece of rubber inner tube was cut to form a loop of the relevant size and elasticity. The locking handle is aligned with the tailstock centre and the loop pulled over both of them.

The whole operation takes only a few seconds and obviates the prising out of the tailstock centre.

I hope this rather simple device will be helpful to some of your readers. Several of my fellow-turners have made use of it and find it effective.

W.L. Briggs, 26 Trajan Walk, Heddon on the Wall, Newcastle upon Tyne.

Every turner will recognise the problem of hunting

96 Tool rack (1)

for tools which are covered with shavings on the bench or under the lathe. Having suffered for too long with this I solved the problem by making a tool rack which allows the shavings to fall through and can be fitted into a drawer when not in use.

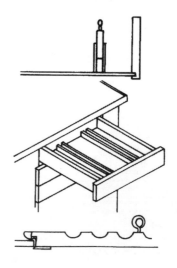

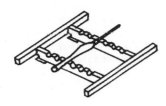

The rack is a simple frame that can be hooked on to the edge of my bench. It is held in position by a length of 25mm 1" quadrant which acts as a hook to fit on a moulding I have fitted round the edge of the bench. This means the rack can be moved to any suitable position round the bench.

I have fitted two runners in a drawer which hold the rack steady and raise it above the base of the drawer so other tools can be stored underneath. There are two large screw eyes in the top of the rack so it can be easily lifted out.

Tony Farmer, 7 St Peter's Road, Ditton, Kent ME20 6PJ.

If you have a bench-mounted lathe, here is a convenient way of keeping your tools handy.

Fix two battens between the legs from side to side, one high at the front and one low at the back. Fix corrugated plastic roofing sheet to the battens so that it slopes steeply downwards.

Bench top.

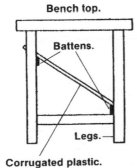

Battens.

Legs.

Corrugated plastic.

Side view.

Each corrugation holds one tool, with a strip of softwood at the bottom to stop the tools sliding too far.

Walter Gundrey, Grange House, Alston, Cumbria CA9 3SL.

98 Tools for a song

People turning on a shoestring like myself, may be interested to hear that I have made a good set of turning tools from old files. (I remember from my schooldays being told by my metalwork master that files are made from the finest tool steel.)

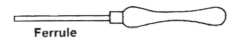

Ferrule

I turn my own handles to suit my hands, making the ferrule out of 22mm copper pipe readily available from DIY stores. Make the ferrule a tight fit, tap it into the handle, then tap the handle on to the tang of the file.

Grind the tip of the file into the shape required. For those more technically minded, the files can be tempered to the correct hardness/toughness.

I bought two 255mm 10" files from a car boot sale for 20p each and the turned the handles from off cuts, thus making two good tools for next to nothing.

B.Edmunds, Sunny Bank, Drefach, Llanelli, Dyfed SA14 7AN.

Although aware of this practice, to avoid accident we must point out the danger of using untreated files. Files used as turning tools must be hardened and tempered before use. This process may be carried out in home workshops and a full description can readily be found in an elementary book on practical mechanics. File steel is very hard and brittle and untreated can readily snap. Please be warned. - Ed.)

99 Trammel gauge for pence

A cheap trammel gauge can be made from a plastic ruler and a map pin.

I bought a cheap clear perspex ruler from Woolworths and then drilled a hole at the end of every 6mm 1/4", 12mm 1/2" and 25mm inch gradation line. Placing the map pin in the zero hole, I can now draw any circle up to a 12" radius. If one has not got a small enough drill, a hot needle will do the trick.

G. Goodman, 24 Waterloo Road, Newport, Gwent NP9 4FP.

100 Two for the price of one

I thought you might like a couple of tips I use in my workshop.

The first is a cost saving.

If you have a lathe with an inboard and outboard spindle, as I have on my ML8, certain tools will be required in both 'hands'.

To cut the dovetail recess in the base of a bowl for my Masterchuck, I am advised to use a 60° scraper. This would mean two tools. My tip is, cut a straight-sided recess with a parting tool or straight-across scraper, then cut the dovetail with a skew chisel, used in scraper mode, ground to the recommended 60°. This can be used either 'hand'. So saving one tool.

The second tip.

I have a vertical drill stand that takes an electric drill.

Unfortunately it has no depth stop.

The simple answer is to turn a hardwood tube

that will fit over the drill pillar, between the carriage and the stand base. Hey presto, one stop. Obviously you could make several to different lengths, or one long one and cut it to length as each job crops up.

Neil F. Poston, 46 Littell Tweed, Chelmsford, Essex CM2 6SH.

101 Two-way depth gauge

The usual depth gauge for use when turning hollowed work is single-acting, but if you make it with square stock it can become two-way. This allows you to set the gauge for one job without disturbing the depth setting for another job.

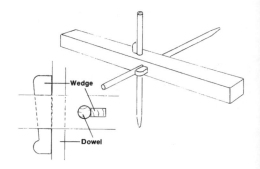

You could set one way to suit the roughed depth, while the other way indicates the finished depth. The two settings could show maximum and minimum allowable depths in production work.

Make the stock from 25mm 1" square hardwood slightly longer than the maximum diameter you expect to turn. Taper and round pieces of 8mm 5/16" dowel rod for the stems.
Make the hardwood wedges 6mm 1/4" thick and give them raised ends so they are unlikely to get lost.

Percy W. Blandford, Quinton House, Newbold-on-Stour, Stratford-upon-Avon, Warwickshire CV37 8UA.

Un-notchable tool rest

Especially when turning small or thin spindles, with lots of fine detail, even the smallest amount of notching on the rest spoils the smooth traverse of the skew.

For the sheer blissful joy of an uninhibited glide along the rest, try topping the rest with a length of alloy tool steel.

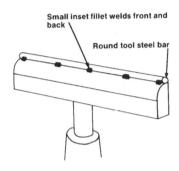

Small inset fillet welds front and back

Round tool steel bar

Sold ready hardened in small standard diameters, usually in 150mm 6" lengths, it may be tacked in position to a mild steel rest, using a small electric welder, without detectably affecting its hardness. On a cast iron rest, Araldite the rod into a ground, filed or machined groove should also do the trick.

I have used 8mm 5/16" dia molybdenum alloy rod tack welded to a Tyme Avon rest and it works very well for me.

Bill Kinsman, 9 Vanity Close, Oulton, Stone, Staffs ST15 8TZ.

103 Waste not...

Here's an idea for saving wax. When I opened a tin of Briwax, I found the contents to be in a lump in the bottom of the tin. This was my own fault for not putting the lid on correctly. I don't like to waste anything, so I thought about what use I could make of the solid piece of Briwax.

I applied it directly to the wood I was working on in the lathe, and then used a soft cloth to polish it. To my delight and amazement the result was excellent. It was a very good shine, maybe even better than when the wax was in a paste form, and of course it saves on a cloth to apply it with.

So my mistake of leaving the lid loose turned out not to be a bad one after all.

Robert A. Peterson, Westview Cottage, West End, Stainforth, Doncaster, South Yorkshire DN7 5SA.

104 Wooden faceplates

We often see wooden gizmos suggested for various special jobs, but they are usually fixed to a metal faceplate. I have found it perfectly satisfactory to make wooden faceplates drilled and tapped to screw directly on to the lathe mandrel.

Mine has a metric thread 24 x 3, and I bought a new second taper tap from a local engineer's supplies store for £5. Had I been able to find the thread to suit my mandrel on a second-hand market stall I expect it would have cost 50p.

Now, when I need a faceplate of a certain size, I just make a wooden one, the dimensions governed by the job. First drill the hole - the size is often stamped on the tap. Next cut the thread, screw on to the mandrel and true

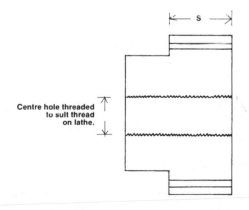

Centre hole threaded to suit thread on lathe.

up. I make the depth S to suit the screws I have. Any diameter is possible - simple and effective.

I got my lathe two years ago from a newspaper advertisement. When I went to collect it, it was in pieces on the floor of an outside loo. The last time I had seen a lathe was at college 50 years before, but I was able to recognise several pieces.

When I got the bits home there were some pieces missing - a base for the bed bars and a banjo for the tool rest - so I made these from wood. I don't know the make of lathe, but the large 3/4 HP motor is German, made by Sachsenwerk in Saxony.

Roy Dodd, 46 Start Bay Park, Strete, Dartmouth, South Devon TQ6 0RY.

105 Work-holding jig

I have designed a device to hold irregular shaped wood for bowl turning without the use of screws

as in the use of a faceplate. It can be built by the woodturner to suit his or her own needs, the size and number of jaws being selected by the builder-user.

The device should be capable of holding work internally and externally and having purpose-built jaws if required. The prototype has six jaws and will hold 305mm 12" projects (see photo).

The 'body' is of MDF, although ply would probably be better, which is screwed to a standard faceplate.

If there is enough interest in the idea, metal parts and construction sketches will be available from Ward Tooling, Units 41 H & I, Bede Industrial Estate, Jarrow, Tyne & Wear NE32 3HG.

Gordon Degg, 19 Birch Avenue, Alsager, Stoke-on-Trent, Staffordshire ST7 2QZ.

The device holding wood to be bored for a clock movement.

Index

	Tip
abrasive paper	
cutting	25
storing	64
anglegrinder	
used to sharpen bandsaw blades	1
Anglepoise lamp	
used to mount collector of dust extractor	48
Axminster chuck	65, 79, 86
bandsaw	
blades, sharpening	1
made mobile with castors	63
mounted on a rotating table	90
bench	
made mobile with castors	63
blanks	
finding centre	11, 13
gluing without sliding	42
making easily	17
bobbin chuck	
made cheaply	2, 3
bowls	
avoiding need for dovetail chuck	17
finding centre of blanks	11, 13
making crosstool holder for	24
marking burr for turning	61
overcoming 'sore' patches	89
thin-walled, using home-made steady	59,87
thin-walled, using tape to stop vibration	41
using template to design	4
bowl-steady	
made cheaply	59, 87
brace and bits	
adapted as turning gouges	80

	Tip
bullnose centre	
adaptor for live centre	5
bumper-outer	
for knocking centres from head- and tailstock	6
burr	
finding centre of gravity	10
marking out for bowls	61
cakes	
icing aid	11
calliper	
double-ended, made cheaply	29
using diameter template instead of	28
carpet tape, double-sided	
used to fix workpiece to faceplate	34
castors	
fitted to lathe, bench etc.	63
centralising tool	
for centring faceplate on blank disc	7, 8
centre drill	
used to minimise splitting	9
used to prepare spindles	75
centre of gravity	
finding for odd-shaped burr	10
centre pin	
knock-out, for fast working	12
centres, finding	
making a centre square	11
making a pocket centre finder for smaller items	74
making centring device for bowl blanks	13
chisel	
grinding at correct angle	43
skew, used to cut a dovetail	99
chisel holder	
rotating, making	82

	Tip
chuck	
compression/expansion, improvement on	66
cup, made from oil filter	37
dovetail, avoiding need for	17
dual-purpose, made from drill chuck	31
for small items	14, 49
four-jaw, protecting against sharp edges	76
jam, improvement on	46
jam, made from cup chuck	44
Multistar, making smaller wooden jaws for	67
pin, an alternative to	73
pin, improved with Rawlbolt	77
screw, made from oil filter	37
three-jaw, for small items, making	49
twin-splined internal, making	73
clothes peg	
used for sanding in tight corners	38
compression/expansion chuck	
improvement on	66
computer monitor arm	
used to mount tool stand	64
concentricity	
maintaining in work removed from lathe	20, 40
copying device	
made cheaply	21
cork	
freezing to aid turning	62
Coronet lathe	22, 51, 70, 79
corrugated plastic	
used as tool rack	96
counters	
made in large numbers	23
Craft Supplies chuck	79
crosstool holder	
for deep bowl turning	24

	Tip
cup chuck	
made from oil filter	37
depth gauge	
two-way, making	100
diameter template	
avoiding need for calliper	28
discs	
finding centre	11, 13
made in large numbers	23
dividing head	
made cheaply	15
dovetail	
cutting without a scraper	99
dovetail chuck	
avoiding need for	17
drill, power	
home-made depth stop for	99
mounted on elastic luggage straps	39
drill, twist	
used for measuring small dimensions	62
drilling	
light pulls without wandering	56, 92
small pieces accurately	54
drill press	
overcoming an inadequate throat	68
duckboard	
for lathe bench	32
dust extractor	
made cheaply	16
made quieter	48
with Anglepoise-mounted collector	48
with multiple inlets	33

	Tip		Tip
faceplate		headstock	
centring on blank disc using home-made tool	7, 8	bumper-outer for knocking out centre	6
fixing to large workpiece	84		
fixing to workpiece without screws	34	indexing plate	
made from pulley	55	making your own	51
making a lever to loosen	35	used as an aid for decorative work	45,50
wooden, fixed directly to lathe mandrel	103		
		jack, scissor	
face visor		used as an aid for handicapped turners	53
cleaning	18		
protecting from sap and resin	19	jam chuck	
removing scratches	18	improvement on	46
		made from cup chuck	44
ferrules			
for tool handles, making	36	jig, work-holding	
		substituted for faceplate	104
file			
adapted as turning tool	97	lacquer	
		saving	85
file, power			
mounted on elastic luggage straps	39	lathe	
		home-made	50
flexi-drill		made mobile with castors	63
mounted on elastic luggage straps	39		
		light cord pulls	
floor		made without drill wander	56, 92
made non-slip with roofing felt	69		
		lighting	
glasses		suggestions for workshop	93
avoiding fogging	27		
		live centre	
glue gun, electric		adapted as bullnose centre	5
used in making jam chucks	44		
		luggage straps, elastic	
gluing		used to mount power drills and files	39
circular blanks, avoiding sliding	42		
		mandrel	
gouge		used for wheel-making	60
adapted from spoon bit and brace	80		
grinding at correct angle	43	masonry bit	
used to make long small tapers	57	used to dress grinding wheel	30
grinding wheel		Masterchuck	57,99
dressing	30		
		measuring	
handles, tool		small dimensions using twist drill	62
making ferrules for	36		

	Tip			Tip
Multistar chuck			roofing felt	
making smaller wooden jaws for	67		used as non-slip floor	69
Myford lathe	23, 78, 99		router	
			setting depth gauge using twist drill	62
nail file			rubber	
used for sanding in tight corners	38		freezing to aid turning	62
non-slip floor			sanding	
made from roofing felt	69		in tight corners	38
			rounded objects	88
oil filter			using flexible drive on power drill	39
used to make chuck	37		without 'sore' patches	89
overall			sanding drums and sticks	
using surgeon's gown as	52		making	83
parting saw			sandpaper	
made from bandsaw blade	70		see abrasive paper	
parting tool			scraper	
made from power saw blade	71		grinding at correct angle	43
made from steel knife blade	72		screw chuck	
pin chuck			made from oil filter	37
alternative to	73		screw threads	
improved with Rawlbolt	77		chasing by hand	47
plastic, corrugated			Sears & Roebuck lathe	75
used as tool rack	96		shape tracer	
polish			improvement on commercial	21
saving	85		small pieces	
pulley			chuck for	14, 49
used to make faceplate	55		drilling accurately	54
			turning between centres	86
Rawlbolt			smock, turner's	
used to improve pin chuck	77		using surgeon's gown as	52
rechucking			spectacles	
a simplified method	79		avoiding fogging	27
Record Power lathe	50			
roller blind				
used to keep workshop cleaner	81			

	Tip		Tip
spindle-puller		tools	
for Coronet lathe	22	adapted from files	97
		see also chisel, gouge, parting tool, scraper	
split turnings			
made without glue	91	trammel gauge	
		made cheaply	98
spoon bit			
adapted as turning gouge	80	turning	
		short pieces between centres	86
surgeon's gown			
used as turner's smock	52	Tyme lathe	86, 101
switch box		Union Jubilee lathe	65
on a sliding fitting for lathe	93		
		visor	
tailstock		see face visor	
bumper-outer for knocking out centre	6		
centre tray for short-bed lathes	94	wax	
		saving	102
tape, masking			
used to stop vibration in thin-walled bowls	41	wheels	
		made quickly with a mandrel	60
tapers			
long and small, made with fingernail gouge	57	Wolfcraft clamp	45
template		workbench	
for diameters	28	made mobile with castors	63
used to design bowls	4		
		work-holding jig	
tenons		substituted for faceplate	104
cutting	26		
		wrench	
tool handles		adapted for cutting tenons	26
making ferrules for	36		
tool rack			
made from corrugated plastic	96		
made to avoid catching shavings	95		
making a rotating chisel holder	82		
using computer monitor arms to mount	64		
toolrest			
adapted to extend capacity at outboard end	65		
made for long pieces between centres	58		
made un-notchable	101		
making a free-standing rear support	78		

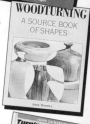